I

SEX
WORKERS

I ❤ **SEX WORKERS**

# A CHRISTIAN RESPONSE TO PEOPLE IN THE SEX TRADE

## LIA CLAIRE SCHOLL

**CHALICE**
PRESS

ST. LOUIS, MISSOURI

Bible quotations, unless otherwise noted, are from the *New Revised Standard Version Bible,* copyright 1989, Division of Christian Education of the National Council of the Churches of Christ in the United States of America. Used by permission. All rights reserved.

Interior design: Scribe Inc.

Visit www.chalicepress.com

10  9  8  7  6  5  4  3  2  1                    12  13  14  15  16  17

PRINT: 9780827216624   EPUB: 9780827216631   EPDF: 9780827216648

**Library of Congress Cataloging-in-Publication Data**

Scholl, Lia Claire.
I heart sex workers : a Christian response to people in the sex trade / by Lia Claire Scholl.
    p. cm.
Includes bibliographical references.
ISBN 978-0-8272-1662-4 (alk. paper)
1. Sex–Religious aspects–Catholic Church. 2. Prostitution–Religious aspects--Catholic Church. 3. Human trafficking. I. Title.
BX1795.S48S36 2012
261.8'331534–dc23
                                     2012019268

# Contents

## SECTION 4: Jesus Was a Harm Reductionist; You Be One, Too

# Introduction

I first noticed an interesting phenomenon after I'd worked with sex workers for a while. Many women who do sex work have high voices. When they leave the industry, their voices often drop an octave.

I heard once in a preaching seminar that a woman should drop her voice a bit to be more soothing to the congregation. But by the time I heard that, I already knew: your voice, your true voice, can't be forced. It can't be prompted. One day, it just shows up. And it can't be silent anymore.

I attended seminary because I'd felt called to ministry since I was thirteen. Because I had no female pastoral role models, I assumed my focus would have to be missions. So I had visions of working with impoverished women who were struggling toward economic justice, walking alongside them in their trials and tribulations, and teaching marketable skills so they could gain independence and financial strength.

I believed that strong women create better community. I believed in economic justice for all. I believed I could change things.

In my second year in school, I trained to start a Christian Women's Job Corps (CWJC) site through the Woman's Missionary Union of the Southern Baptist Convention. CWJC was a program that supported women getting out of poverty with individualized resources, mentoring, and job skill training. It was a perfect fit for fighting economic injustice.

Seminary for me was a hard road. In the school I attended, there were 180 students, and only 11 of them were women. It was not infrequent that I would have a conversation with other students who would say things like, "You can't be a minister! You're a girl!" Even some of the professors would interpret biblical texts as favoring "differing roles" for women, insisting that they could not be pastors or leaders in the church.

Along the way, I fell in love with pastoring. I love digging deep into the scripture; writing sermons; preaching; planning worship; visiting hospitals; sitting with people; and participating in potlucks, leadership, administration, and funerals and weddings.

One Saturday while I was still in seminary, a friend called to invite me to a strip club. She and her boyfriend would go to one of the local clubs, pay for lap dances, sit at the stages tipping the dancers, and have a good time. My response was an indignant, "No!" I am sure that I said something about the inequality of the power struggles that kept women enslaved to men. My girlfriend responded, "Come on! It'll be fun!" I didn't go.

Soon after graduation, a friend from the CWJC program asked if I would consider using their model to work with individuals in the sex industry, specifically with women who were working in strip clubs. With fear and trepidation, I visited my first strip club.

A Baptist minister who moonlighted as a corrections officer explained the mores of the club. He taught me to focus on the people at the club, to study them, keeping an eye on the customers, noticing where management and the bouncers were, and especially reading the dancers. He trained me to pay deep attention. He emphasized the importance of noticing when someone was using drugs or might be just a little pregnant. Learning to read people helped me be available to their needs and to not be surprised at anything.

Frankly, my first visit was exciting. I was finally seeing the reality of what I'd been trained for, and the injustice to me was obvious. Being there brought up all the indignation and anger I felt from seminary, the sense of entitlement the men seemed to have over the women, and the sense of subservience the women exhibited. What did I notice? The dancers were sitting with customers, and the men were meting out dollar bills to them. Some dancers were on the stage, with their eyes closed, seemingly ignoring the customers. Other women were giving private dances, curling their bodies around the poles, looking bored. I interpreted what I saw as the women being victimized by the men; the men were the ones with money, and the women needed to use their sexuality to get that money.

I started Star Light Ministries with the mission to share "unconditional love and friendship with women who are exotic dancers so they will not forget they are also loved and valued by God. We help them build supportive communities and find resources for successful living."

Ah, the immaturity of youth!

Six months into Star Light's existence, it seemed I didn't understand something about the culture of the clubs. Perhaps my reading of who had power and who didn't have power was skewed by my own experience. Perhaps there was more going on in the club than I understood.

How could I understand the exchange, both financial and sexual, that took place in the interactions? Learning about that exchange has taken me places I did not think I'd go, from strip clubs in Las Vegas to sex blogger parties in New York, from Christian conferences against prostitution to conferences put on by sex workers and their allies.

I've worked with individuals who have traded sex for over twelve years. I've listened to their stories. I've sat by their side in pain and suffering. I've celebrated marriages with them. I've cried with them. I've tested them for HIV and sat with them in hospital rooms. I've held their children. I've laughed with them. I've mourned with them and for them.

Because I'm a minister—and candid about it—I've faced the stigma that comes with being an ally, especially a Christian ally, to people engaged in sex work. Sex workers often encounter do-gooders who want to rescue them from their situations. Because other Christians offer judgment, moralism, and evangelism, they expect those same attitudes from me. They expect me to be a "Captain-Save-a-Ho," a person who tries to rescue and change sex workers. When I don't try to "save" the people I meet, just be their friend, over and over, they express surprise.

I've learned that trust is a difficult thing to build and an easy thing to lose. Because sex workers have faced so many judgmental do-gooders, they find it difficult to trust Christians. But even when a Christian overcomes those obstacles, one misstep can ruin all the trust. One Sunday afternoon I visited a club and the manager came over to my table. He was upset because someone had left evangelistic tracts in the men's room of the club. He asked if we had left them. I explained that it wasn't us, that the tactic of dropping tracts seemed underhanded, and apologized that someone had distributed them.

Along the way, sex workers changed in my mind from being the people I *ministered to* to the people I *loved.* I began to understand why Jesus said, in John 15:15, "I no longer call you servants . . . Instead, I call you friends." I came to understand that a relationship of mutuality is required in ministry, that if I am going to be true to people, then the truest I can be is to be open to listen, to seek to understand their experience, to learn from them rather than feeling I have something to teach. Some time ago, my relationships with sex workers moved from being one-way to being mutual, from "I have the help you need" to "We can be here for one another."

Because of this, sex work has become very personal to me. There are people I love working in strip clubs, advertising their services online, and offering sex for sale. It is my sincere hope that these individuals will be treated better tomorrow than they are today. It is my hope that they will not face the stigma, economic disenfranchisement, and isolation that so often comes with sex work.

After Star Light, I worked at HIPS (Helping Individual Prostitutes Survive), a harm reduction organization in Washington, D.C., whose mission is to assist people who trade sex in leading healthier lives. At HIPS I was the client advocacy program manager and responsible for HIV testing and counseling, a program for individuals who had been arrested for solicitation, a twenty-four-hour hotline, and case management for our 225 in-house clients.

And while I have worked with men who trade sex, the majority of my experience is with women, including transgender women. Transgender individuals are people who identify with a gender that differs from the sex they were assigned at birth. Women are the overwhelming majority of sex workers and the most vulnerable.

I have written this book to help you understand the sex trade without having to log the hours of counseling women, visit strip clubs, pass out condoms on the street, or sit in a courtroom as a woman gets arraigned on prostitution charges. I have also written this book to combat the idea that the sex trade can be easily understood and solved, as the antitrafficking and profamily movement will lead you to believe. It is my hope that since you picked up this book, you already care about sex workers. You have already heard that the individuals out there who are trading sex need allies.

I have also written this book to help you avoid making the same mistakes I did. I'm writing not so much to help you but to help sex workers avoid the kind of judgmental things Christians and other do-gooders unwittingly do.

I hope you will, after reading this book, understand the systemic reasons why people enter the sex industry. I hope you will also understand the forces that make exiting the industry difficult, at best. I hope you will become an ally to sex workers, whether through direct care, advocacy, or friendship. At the very least, I hope you will be more empathetic and understanding of their social location and more able to offer acceptance and compassion.

The Bible suggests that judgment and punishment are not the correct response to sex work. The writer of the book of Hosea says,

> I will not punish your daughters when they play the
> whore,
> nor your daughters-in-law when they commit adultery;

for the men themselves go aside with whores,
and sacrifice with temple prostitutes;
thus a people without understanding comes to ruin.
(Hosea 4:14)

This verse suggests that our response should be one of understanding—of both the forces that lead women into sex work and the way the sex industry works—not so much to close the industry down but to make sure that every person in the sex industry has choices.

Ultimately, Jesus expects us to love our neighbors as ourselves and to love our enemies. People in the sex industry are our neighbors. They may also be our enemies, but in order to love them, we must first understand them.

As I write this, I've just had word that a twenty-three-year-old transgender woman, a previous client of mine, was shot and killed. I do not know if she was killed because she was in the sex industry, nor do I know if it's because she was trans. I do know the level of violence individuals in the sex industry face is, in large part, because of the discrimination and isolation they face. Because portions of the sex industry are illegal, the individuals who are trading sex do not have the protection of the police.

Unfortunately, these deaths are far too common. I would like to dedicate this book to Lashay and the other women I have known who have been beaten, abused, sexually assaulted, and killed due to their experience in the sex industry. Until the violence ends, this world will not be whole.

*Section 1*
*Falling, Jumping, or Getting Pushed:*
*Why People Enter Sex Work*

# Tamar's Story

## *Playing the Harlot*

My father-in-law once said to me–just after he yelled, "Burn her at the stake!"–"You are more righteous than I."*

This is the story of how it happened and what I did to warrant both his wrath and his praise.

My family is Canaanite, and my father is a farmer who lives close to the Kanah Brook. My mother passed away when I was very young. My father is always at odds with me, as I haven't always been a good daughter. I don't like to do the dishes or sweep our home. Instead, I like to create with fabrics, paint with the pigments from plants, or just get lost in daydreaming.

My father is an astute business man in addition to being a farmer, and when he decided that I was ready to marry, he called the local Jewish leader. My father and our family converted to Judaism so that my father would have access to more Jewish families to buy the feed he sold. Our local priest had ties with the family of Avraham and Yaakov, who were the forefathers of our community, and my father greatly wanted to make those connections; he wanted access to their flocks.

Yehuda, one of the children of Yaakov, lived in our part of the country. He had three sons, all from a Canaanite mother. Her family was close with my family, and her three sons were named Er, Onan, and Shelah.

My father arranged my marriage to Er. He asked if I approved of the arrangement, and not wanting to disappoint him, I said, "Of

* The opening of each section of this book is midrash, a retelling and filling-in-of-details of Bible stories.

course." But I didn't. I'm an independent spirit, and I was scared that a husband would not let me be free, that I would have a life of sweeping and washing dishes.

Our first months of marriage were pleasant, given that we were both so young and we had not yet consummated the marriage. We played together as brother and sister. I had the time and freedom I needed to sew, to paint, to daydream. But then the time for childishness was over.

Around this time, Er's mean streak became evident. Our time together was no longer playful. Instead, it was forceful. In bed, my husband insisted on anal sex only, and it was painful. When I told him it hurt, he insisted it was the only way. When I said I wanted to get pregnant, he would laugh bitterly and say, "I don't want children with you."

Er also became angry and hateful in other areas of our life. He had rules for everything. When I didn't meet his standards, he would make me pay. He would slap me for not cleaning the house. One time, he kicked me out of the house for a day because I didn't sweep the floor.

And then, unexpectedly, he died. My best friend said, "God must have hated him."

According to Jewish tradition, a widow with no children was given in marriage to her husband's closest male relative. When the widow conceived a child, that child would inherit the wealth of the original husband, and the widow would keep a place in society. Yehuda decided to give me in marriage to the second son, Onan. Onan already had a wife who he loved very much. Her name was Rebecca, and she wasn't very happy with me "taking her man." But it was Onan's duty, and she ensured that he did it poorly. Rebecca hadn't had children, so she insisted that Onan not give me children. Onan came to my bedroom, but he didn't have sex with me. Instead, he masturbated over me, spilling his seed on the ground. He didn't perform his duty.

Then Onan died. My best friend said, "Serves him right." It's good to have friends.

After the burial and the appropriate time of mourning, Yehuda called me to him. "Tamar, what am I going to do with you?" he asked. "I've given you my eldest sons in marriage, and they are dead. Maybe you are not good for my family. Because it is my responsibility to give you my third son, I will, but he is very young. Until he is ready, I would like you to return to your father's house and play the widow."

So I headed home to father, who expected that I would work, cleaning, scrubbing, or sweeping. No more time for daydreaming.

My father became gravely ill. Because of the way that land rights in our country work, my brother stood to inherit the farm. My brother has a mean streak much like Er's and a wife who is meaner and cannot stand me.

I was headed to ruin. I could not marry again, because Yehuda required that I "play the widow," and I seriously doubted that he would have ever given me in marriage to Shelah. Yehuda held me responsible for the death of his two sons.

As I was carrying water one noontime, I saw a young woman in the distance. It was obvious, even to me, that she was selling sex. She was making eye contact with men—women don't do that in our town—and the veil she wore shone in the sunlight, a brazen display that the plain people of my town don't engage in. She was different, and I liked the difference.

After seeing her a few times, I walked over to her and asked, "Have you been doing this long?"

"Not too long," she said. She introduced herself as Aderet.

When I asked why she did this work, she said, "For a better life."

"This is a better life?" I asked.

"It's better than relying on one man to help me. It's better than fighting the abuse that one man can do. It's better than giving in."

And I felt it deep inside me: my way out.

Yehuda's wife had died, and I knew he would be seeking some companionship as a result. I knew that Yehuda attended the sheep sheering at Timnah each year. I decided to meet him there in the hopes of seducing him and getting pregnant.

But first, I received a few tips from Aderet. The first lesson was that appearances count. I had to adopt a new persona, a new walk, a new talk. And although my father-in-law had never seen me naked, I knew I would have to look different as well. Aderet said that once I was in the appointment, the client would be unlikely to recognize me. She said many times clients didn't even look at you.

Second, I needed a way for Yehuda to pay me. My friend was paid with whatever the client traded. She then had a broker who sold those things for her. Some might call the man her pimp, but she called him a friend. And he left her with a good living wage. It was not my intention to take money for this. Instead, I wanted a child, and a way to prove to Yehuda that he was the father.

Third, Aderet told me, you have to remember not to fall in love. "It's hard," she said, "because we all want to be loved."

I knew that would not be a problem.

It took me a couple of weeks, but I prepared. I got skin treatments, mud baths from the Dead Sea. I put henna in my hair to give it a different shine. I lost a few pounds to help with the disguise. I made myself a new veil and a dress to match it.

I was ready.

I waited for Yehuda by a small tent on the road. I could tell when he was coming by his entourage. When he got close, I stepped outside. I cleared my throat. He looked over. Then came the hard part: I had to seduce him with only my eyes. Everything else was covered in red.

It worked!

Step one was negotiating the price. Yehuda offered a young goat from his flock. I accepted but said, "What will you give me as a pledge?" He gave me his seal, cord, and staff, and these would prove that any child from this union was his. He never noticed the irony. In Hebrew, the word for seal, *hotam*, sounds like *hatan*, which means father-in-law. And cord? *Petil*, which sounds like *peti*, means simpleton.

My friend had warned me that the seduction lasts longer than the few moments of sex. Instead, it is the time the client is with you that matters. So we talked, me with my new voice. He told me about his sorrows of the last few years, the loss of his sons and his wife. He told me about his son, the trip to Timnah, and his small flock that year.

It was sad. I could feel his pain.

Then we moved to the bed. It wasn't like with Er. It wasn't angry or mean. It wasn't like Onan, which was sort of like I wasn't there. It was gentle and kind.

After it was over, I packed up and went home, put on my widow's clothing, and tried not to think about it.

Four weeks later, the vomiting made me think about it again. Within a few weeks of having sex with my father-in-law, I was showing symptoms of being pregnant.

As happy as I was, my father had become very sick. Six weeks into my pregnancy, he took to his bed never to get out again. I tended him, bringing him food and wine, feeding him, making him comfortable. Toward the end, on a bright early morning, my father grabbed my arm as I was straightening his covers. "Tamar," he whispered, "come closer. I want to bless you."

"Father," I cried, "I don't deserve your blessing. I have been a bad daughter."

"My sweet girl," he said, "You may not have been a great daughter, but you have been a wonderful woman. Your life is hard, and you have faced it with courage and conviction. May the God we serve give you the strength to face what comes next, because you will need courage and conviction."

He died not long after that. I wrapped him in burial clothes and anointed his body with oils. I said my good-byes.

Meanwhile, I grew bigger and bigger as my pregnancy progressed. The time had come to go to my father-in-law's home.

It's hard, in a community like ours, to keep secrets. I had hoped to return to Yehuda's home quietly, but the women from his community saw me, and they ran to tell their husbands that I was returning—pregnant.

In my situation, being pregnant was a visible sign of the biggest sin I could commit. I was considered a married woman, even though I was not married to the youngest son and the older sons were dead. My pregnancy was a sign of adultery, and adultery is a sin punishable by death.

I grabbed one of Yehuda's servants. "Please, tell your master that I am here," I said. The servant led me to waiting quarters.

The servant came back and said, "Yehuda has spoken and said, 'She has played the harlot! Have her burned to death.'"

I implored the servant, "Please, take this seal, this cord, and this staff, and tell Yehuda that I am pregnant by the man who owns these."

After presenting these items to Yehuda, the servant came to retrieve me. He brought me in front of Yehuda, who was surrounded by his most trusted advisors. "She is more righteous than I, since I wouldn't give her to my son Shelah. She shall live in my home as my wife, and I will be father to her child."

Which was it? Was I righteous? Or did I "play the harlot"? Or was it both? I didn't know. But oh, my relief! And then surprise, as I learned I was to bear children! I gave birth to twins, Perez and Zerah.

We did live as husband and wife, but we never shared a bed again. Yehuda was old, and having children again gave his older years a fullness that didn't require sex. Frankly, I was thankful for the freedom and the time to dream.

I remained friends with Aderet. She would come visit me regularly. She continued to trade sex, and she always seemed to be happy. I never told anyone how we met . . .

\*   \*   \*

What do you think of Tamar? Do you think that she is a manipulative bitch who tricked her father-in-law into having sex with her? It would be easy to interpret Tamar in this light. She doesn't get what she wants, so she fixes herself up, lies about her identity, and seduces Yehuda.

But that's not how the Bible interprets her. In the Torah, a woman who is named is important, a woman whose story is told is more important, and a woman who is the ancestor of David is even more important. Of course, Tamar is not just the ancestor of David. She's also the ancestor of Jesus—and named as such in Matthew—which marks her as a righteous woman.

Why would she be considered a heroine, and why would Yehuda say that she is more righteous than he? At this time in the history of the Jews, it is important to understand that the Law hasn't been given yet. Moses hadn't yet climbed the mountain to get the tablets of the Ten Commandments. However, their religion, norms, and mores had already begun to be formulated. So even though there is no law about taking care of widows, there is the beginning of tradition.

Tamar's story can be judged in light of the law. Deuteronomy 25:5–6 says,

> When brothers reside together, and one of them dies and has no son, the wife of the deceased shall not be married outside the family to a stranger. Her husband's brother shall go in to her, taking her in marriage, and performing the duty of a husband's brother to her, and the firstborn whom she bears shall succeed to the name of the deceased brother, so that his name may not be blotted out of Israel.

This is called levirate marriage, and Tamar is the first woman to marry her "kinsman redeemer" in the Hebrew Bible. The purpose of levirate marriage is to create an heir for the dead husband, Er. It goes a little further, though, than an heir for Er. It's also financial security and societal standing for the widow. And while externally, Onan seems to take on the levirate responsibility, he certainly abdicates that responsibility through "spilling his seed."

So it's important for Tamar to get pregnant because pregnancy (and a son, especially) will give Tamar her independence, or at least her self-sufficiency. If she has a child, she doesn't need a man to take care of her; she can take care of herself.

It is ultimately Yehuda's responsibility that Tamar is provided for through the birth of a son. He has only one son left who could marry Tamar, but Yehuda waits. Waiting is certainly understandable. To him, Tamar could be a black widow who is killing his sons, or it could be plain old coincidence. Would he want to risk his only remaining son, Shelah? Perhaps he wouldn't want to risk Shelah, but Yehuda could marry Tamar too. The father-in-law could also be the kinsman redeemer.[1] But Yehuda ducks his responsibility, leaving Tamar childless, defenseless, and alone.

Yehuda's response still leaves Tamar with very few options.

Tamar, taking matters into her own hands, refuses to accept her lack of security and acts as an agent of change through performing sex work.

A few months after having sex with an unknown prostitute on the road to Timnah, Yehuda learns that Tamar is pregnant. When he finds this out, he orders her death! Leaving off the discussion of the hypocrisy involved given that he had visited a sex worker, the speed at which Yehuda decides Tamar's death by violence is stunning.

Although Tamar is accused of prostitution, it's not the sex work that seems to upset everyone. It's her marital status. If she were unmarried, it wouldn't look good, but it is complicated by the fact that she is promised to one of Yehuda's sons. It's not just sex work but adultery and fornication.

Yehuda learns that the he is responsible for Tamar's pregnancy, backs off the punishment, and actually commends Tamar. "She is more righteous than I." This Hebrew phrase, "*Tzadkah mimeni,*" means "more right" and "than I am" or "from me."[2] And then he takes Tamar into his family. She is the heroine of the story for standing up for her rights; for overcoming the oppression of her caste, gender, and race; and for becoming the agent of change in her own life. Tamar builds a future for herself and she becomes the great-great-great-great-grandmother of the Messiah.

The comparison to modern-day sex work is simple: people enter sex work because of the lack of justice in their given society. It doesn't matter if it's New York City or Elkton, Tennessee, Bangkok, Thailand or Kolkata, India. It doesn't matter if the person is sixteen years old or fifty-two. The lack of viable choices drives people into sex work.

The sixteen-year-old who has left a bad situation at home has few choices. The fifty-two-year-old who has been left bankrupt by her husband of twenty-five years has few choices. The teenage girl in Thailand who has left her home in Cambodia for a better life has few choices. Society owes people more choices than it provides.

What if we begin to see the people who engage in sex work as individuals who are seeking their own paths in an unjust world? What if we see them as agents of change in their own lives? What if we begin to see them as seeking justice and fighting oppression?

Regardless of the nobility and heroism that might have gone into Tamar's choice, it could have ended differently. Where Tamar faced being burned to death, folks today face violence, whether physical, sexual, emotional, or intellectual. Choosing sex work can mean incarceration, hunger, poverty, homelessness, joblessness, mental illness, rape, or even death.

It is our responsibility, as Christians seeking justice in the world, to build more choices for individuals who choose sex work because of the unjust choices they have to endure. In order to do this, we first have to recognize our biases surrounding sex work. We then have to recognize the forces that make sex work a viable choice for individuals—and fight to change those oppressive conditions. Finally, we have to seek to make this path that people have chosen as safe as possible while offering options for leaving.

# 1

## Girls, Girls, Girls

### *Media and Cultural Portrayals*

Long legs and burgundy lips

—MOTLEY CRÜE

In Genesis 38 we find Yehuda jumping to the conclusion that Tamar "played the harlot." He had a whole list of assumptions that came along with that presupposition. We do the same thing today. We have assumptions about people engaged in sex work, formed mostly from mainstream media but also by the antitrafficking movement that dominates the discussion around prostitution.

Mainstream media use certain words to bring up negative pictures in our minds. In news reports, they'll use hooker, stripper, call girl, and a myriad of other names, all of which bring up images of streetwalkers with a lot of skin showing. Think Julia Roberts in *Pretty Woman* when she's walking the street: thigh high boots, a very short skirt, and a top that reveals her stomach and cleavage.

When asked what comes into their minds when they hear the word "prostitute," HIPS (Helping Individual Prostitutes Survive) volunteers gave the following descriptions:

- slut
- whore
- hooker
- working girl
- streetwalker

- member of the oldest profession
- tart
- escort
- hustler
- scarlet woman
- tramp
- ho
- bitch
- wench
- rent boy
- temptress
- dirty girl
- stripper
- cam girl
- perv
- show girls

Those are the nice ones. Here are other words that they conjured up:

- drugs
- HIV/AIDS
- sexually transmitted infections
- herpes
- sexually abused
- dirty

The volunteers also reflected on what prostitutes do:

- sell her body
- tempt (especially otherwise blameless individuals)
- demean
- exotic/erotic dance
- massage

I've found that when people talk in depth about those who trade sex, we use phrases like "that homewrecker," "those people, what a pity," or "bless her heart, she doesn't understand how harmful it is to be selling her body." We might even be gracious: "There but for the grace of God go I." Ministers say they want to be "a voice for the voiceless." The words may sound right and proper, but we use all these phrases to separate ourselves from people who trade sex because we don't really understand them. We wouldn't want anyone to think that we could ever do that.

What's really behind these phrases? What words or pictures come to your mind when you think about people who are trading sex? Do you see stiletto heels, short skirts, big wigs, and tight shirts? Do you see a particular race? What about drug use? And what do you envision happens in a client interaction?

Are those pictures helpful?

### Homewrecker

I have heard many stories of wives calling exotic dancers, after finding their phone numbers in their husbands' pockets, and saying, "You've stolen my husband!" I have yet to meet a sex worker who lured a man into sex he didn't want.

Frankly, they don't want your man; they want his money. If a man is found in a "compromising" position, we often absolve him of responsibility by blaming the woman he's with, whether she's a sex worker or a housewife down the street. When we blame the sex worker, we exonerate the man from his responsibility and we really shift the blame to someone who, while maybe not blameless, probably hasn't gone to the trouble of luring the man into the relationship.

### Bless Her Heart

I'm a Southern woman. As such, one of the things we say regularly is, "Bless her/his heart." Everybody knows we're really being condescending and demeaning. We want to appear to have compassion and understanding, and yet we don't. It's like the parable of the Pharisee and the publican in Luke 18:9–14, where the Pharisee looks at the praying tax collector and says, "Thank you, God, that I am not like that person!"

Instead of saying, "Bless her heart," we need to understand more so we can say, "I know that given the same opportunities and the same challenges, I might have made similar decisions."

### There but for the Grace of God Go I

Years ago, Oprah Winfrey interviewed a sex worker. After she finished with the interview, she turned to the audience and said this very phrase.

It's not meant to be degrading, but if you deconstruct it, it says, "I have the grace of God. Therefore God saved me from sex work and didn't save you." How do we presume to know who has the grace of God? And couldn't someone have grace and still enter sex work?

Of course Oprah meant to say, "You and I are the same, and but for circumstances beyond my control, I would have made similar choices and been in a similar place." That is a statement of acceptance, equality, and understanding.

God withholds grace from no one.

## A Voice for the Voiceless

I was talking to a pastor with a large online following. He was interviewing female pastors and said, "I want to give you all a voice." I cleared my throat. I thought, *I already have a voice. It's just that no one wants to listen.*

Many anti–sex work and rescue organizations say that they want to be a "voice for the voiceless." I've never met a sex worker without a voice. What's meant is, "I want to stand with the less powerful," but what's actually said is, "You need someone to speak for you because you are not able/willing/capable of speaking for yourself."

Sex workers do not need someone to be a voice for them; they need individuals to listen to their voices. There's an assumption that individuals who have been trafficked do not have a voice, too. That's not true. They do have voices and opinions about their situations, and many times, they can speak for themselves. However, most times, organizations speak for them.

There's an irony in that I, having never worked in the field, would write a book about sex work where I recommend that we allow space for sex workers to speak for themselves. For now, it's a matter of access. I have access to sex workers' stories and their lives, and I have access to the audience of this book. I hope to act as a bridge for sex workers' stories.

Before I get up to preach a sermon, I always pray, "May the words of my mouth and the meditations of my heart be pleasing to you, O God, my Rock and my Redeemer." That's my goal in writing this book as well. I hope that my words would be honest about my friends and show love. My purpose isn't to give sex workers a voice but to share what I know from listening to them.

## She Doesn't Understand Her Own Experience

When Mel Gibson's movie *The Passion of the Christ* came out, a lot of Jews said it was anti-Semitic and brought up recollections of pogroms (violent riots) in Germany, which oftentimes had passion plays as precursors. A lot of Christians claimed the movie was not anti-Semitic. Which group could best discern whether the movie was anti-Semitic?

When women do get the chance to talk about positive experiences in sex work, they're often criticized by feminist groups. Why? Feminists will explain that individuals who are subordinate begin to trust the system that oppresses them and cannot understand their own experience because they can't see it without the lens of subordination. When someone says of another, "She doesn't understand her own experience," they're saying she cannot be trusted to understand her own occupation; she can't understand she's enslaved. I disagree.

Oppressed people know they are oppressed. Usually they begin to rise up and fight the oppression. There is no doubt that some sex workers are oppressed, beaten, raped, and robbed. And when a sex worker tells me that she's had that experience, I believe her.

But there are others who have not been beaten, raped, or robbed. Even if they have been victims of abuse, the benefits still outweighed the costs for them. When a sex worker tells me she's had *that* experience, I believe her.

Sex work may be enslavement to one woman, but it may be liberation to another. The most liberating thing, for any woman, is to have her experience affirmed and believed, because women can be trusted.

## Selling Her Body

If I could eliminate just one of the phrases, it would be this one. Think about it: "Selling her body." Can a person really *sell* her body? No. You can't sell your body. It remains your possession.

People use the phrase to communicate the *transaction* that occurs. And someone is, indeed, paying another person to perform sex. So why not say "selling sex" instead?

What I really dislike is about this phrase is that "selling your body" denotes a loss of *agency*, as though sex work is about giving up your body. Just because someone is being paid to perform a sex act doesn't mean she is not in control or ownership of her body. This is a critical distinction we must fight for if we're to change people's perception about sex workers. In fact, those who give over control (or have it wrenched from them) are likely to be victimized. That is not sex work; it's victimization. It's important to understand that sex workers, like all of us, have the right, the ability, and the voice to consent and refuse sex at any time. And none of them willingly "sell their bodies."

The client paying for sex is not the "owner" of the sex worker or her body. They aren't even "renting" it because it is never theirs. The client who believes he's attained ownership over the sex worker is grossly mistaken and dangerous.

Mainstream entertainment shares much of the blame for giving us this image of sex workers. In *Pretty Woman*, Vivian (played by Julia Roberts) is a street-level, survival sex worker who gets picked up by a man in a Maserati and is whisked away from her terrible life that was devoid of fancy restaurants, expensive clothing, and shopping sprees. Edward (played by Richard Gere) takes her from the street, and instead of being treated like dirt on her stroll (where she works), she gets to be treated like dirt in the posh shops on Rodeo Drive or by Edward's colleague. Instead of working the street, she gets to be with an emotionally stunted man who believes money is the true measure of a life and who, despite his fear of heights, chooses the uppermost floor in hotels because it is a reminder of his wealth.

Women swooned when Vivian, in her purple ball gown, said to Edward, "I would have stayed for two thousand," to which he responded, "I would have paid four." How cute. This movie painted the prostitute as smart, funny, and beautiful, with rescue as the goal and ultimate prize in sex work.

I'm sure you can tell, but it's so far from the truth of sex work it's painful to me. There are plenty of smart, funny, and beautiful sex workers, but most are not waiting to be rescued by their customers, nor are they as naïve and simplistic as Roberts and Gere. This is not a movie about sex work. It's a fairy tale.

There are other mainstream entertainment portrayals of sex workers. Tina Fey is a comedienne known to be tough on sex work. In a 2009 interview in *Vanity Fair*, Fey said, "I love to play strippers and to imitate them. I love using that idea for comedy, but the idea of actually going there? I feel like we all need to be better than that. That industry needs to die, by all of us being a little bit better than that."[1] In her 2011 book, *Bossypants*, Fey writes, "Politics and prostitution have to be the only jobs where inexperience is considered a virtue. In what other profession would you brag about not knowing stuff?"[2]

This is funny stuff, within reason. But it can be hurtful, too. Chris Rock does a comedy routine about becoming a new father. He says, "Sometimes I am walking with my daughter, I'm talking to my daughter, I'm looking at her, I'm pushing her in the stroller. And sometimes I pick her up and I just stare at her and I realize my only job in life is to keep her off the pole."[3] Parents of sex workers everywhere probably cringe when he says that.

But worst of all are the jokes about violence toward sex workers. In the television show *30 Rock*, starring Tina Fey, Jack Donaghy (played by Alec Baldwin) is in his office, mourning the change in General Electric's ownership. "This is where we used to hold retirement parties. The balcony below is probably still littered with stripper bones."[4] Facebook jokesters post fan pages about killing sex workers. It's all in good fun until it's not, and violence against sex workers happens all too often.

Of course, mainstream entertainment and media are not the only influencers of our negative image of sex workers. The antitrafficking brigade prefers victim language for sex workers. These words include prostituted person (meaning that someone else is prostituting them—that they cannot be doing this to themselves), trafficked person, and "girls exploited by sex traffickers."[5] Victim language denotes that these individuals do not have any choice, any agency in the decisions that brought them to their current position.

Some people are trafficked for sex. Some are forced, coerced, and made to submit to managers, pimps, and traffickers. Sometimes circumstances leave no choice but a bad one. But many people in sex work are just that, people in sex work. They haven't been forced. This was a choice they made. It's not an easy choice, but it's theirs.

If an individual made a choice to get there, she must be the one to make a choice to get out. That's key. If we are only interested in the small minority of "victims," we miss the larger picture and rob them of the dignity of being seen as fully autonomous and free individuals, able to make other choices.

But why does it even matter what we think and how we talk about sex workers? Why is it important to frame our language as respectful? For much of the same reason we've changed from calling people black or negro to African American. Words matter. If we are flippant about the words we use, we will tend to be flippant about the way we treat people.

Those same HIPS volunteers who voiced seedy images like "slut," "streetwalker," and "temptress" when we asked them about the word "prostitute" responded differently when we asked them to consider the term "sex worker." These were the phrases that they came up with:

- professional
- making a living

- paying taxes
- job

See the difference? There's a level of dignity the phrase "sex worker" provides. When we are educated about the matter, our language around sex work changes.

The people we're talking about are people. They brush their teeth in the morning. They develop crushes on other people. They laugh and cry like all of us. They love their children and their nieces and nephews. These are individuals who relate in the world to other people, just as you relate to them. They are daughters and sons, mothers and fathers, sisters and brothers, friends, coworkers, community members, and even members of faith communities. They are loved by God as much as any person in the world.

And God isn't cringing at them. We are.

Probably the most realistic movie I've ever seen starring a sex worker was *The Wrestler*, with Marisa Tomei playing an exotic dancer in a dive bar. Although Marisa Tomei looks great in the movie, you see that she is hustling to make all her money, even putting up with some ridicule and frustration from a young bachelor's party. When Ram (Mickey Rourke) steps in to "save" her from the customers, she gets very angry with him, pointing out that this is her living. Marisa Tomei was nominated for an Academy Award for this role.

Sometimes media campaigns also have positive images. Recently, a Canadian sex work organization called Stepping Stones did a photo campaign where a photo of a young woman said, "I'm glad my prostitute made me finish school." A photo of an elderly woman said, "I'm proud of my tramp, raising two kids on her own." A photo of a young man said, "At my wedding, my younger hooker gave the funniest speech."[6]

For everything else their jobs might be, it's still work, which means each of them feels like you and I do at our jobs. Some days we like it, some days we don't. Some days it's fulfilling, other days it's not.

If it was supposed to be fun all the time, they wouldn't call it work.

Let's hear it for the voiceless homewreckers who don't understand their own oppression while selling their bodies! Bless their hearts! It matters the way we think and speak about sex workers. It will impact those who trade sex and help to remove the stigma attached to the work. And to really have an impact, ultimately, we need to learn more about the true reality of trading sex and, at the very least, get out of the way of sex workers claiming the power to express their voices.

# 2

## Her Strut

### It's All about Agency

But oh they love to watch her strut

—Bob Seger

This is a short chapter with a big point. The only way to improve someone's situation long-term is to fight to increase her agency.

Agency is defined as the capacity of individuals to exert power in their own lives. Humans trafficked for sex do not have the capacity to exert power. They do not have agency. Children do not have agency. A woman who is forced to go out on the street and pay a pimp with the money she has earned has very little agency. Addiction can take away agency. Poverty can take away agency. Injustice can take away agency.

But there are many sex workers who do have agency. They are people who have decided to make money in the sex industry, who have chosen to do this work. They may have other choices but this is their preferred one. Some have made this choice so they can schedule their work in order to stay home with their children. Some have made this choice because they can make more money than they can make in more traditional jobs. Some have made this choice because they enjoy it.

It's important to recognize that agency is a continuum, and sex workers can be found at any level on that continuum. The continuum does not stay the same from day to day. A person can find his or her agency changed in a matter of day or weeks.

So what are the factors that influence agency? Everything.

- age
- gender
- location
- socioeconomic status
- education
- race
- belief
- orientation
- class
- language
- literacy
- transportation
- housing
- family
- drug use
- relationships
- history
- family
- abuse

There are so many factors. Everything is overdetermined, meaning that there are so many factors in each decision, untangling them is impossible. But let's try to untangle a few of them anyway.

The strongest factor in determining agency is whether or not a person believes they have agency. People who believe they have agency tend to exert power in their own lives. People who believe themselves incapable of exerting power tend not to.

Let's take a couple of factors and examine the agency the person has in that situation.

Here's Bobbie. She's sixty-seven years old and retired. She has a mortgage on her home that she can afford but just barely. She drives a ten-year-old vehicle that breaks down sometimes, and she has rheumatoid arthritis that keeps her from getting out of bed two or three days a month. She would really like to move south to live closer to her kids.

What's the most obvious factor that keeps Bobbie from moving south? Well, it's probably money. Bobbie is on a fixed income that keeps her strapped into a house she can barely afford. What are other factors? Well, her age may keep her from working if she decides to get a job. There are very few companies that will hire people older than retirement age. Her illness factors in, too. But what about being female? That may have hurt her—she may have made less money than a man and worked fewer years toward retirement if she stayed home to watch the kids.

But what are some factors that help her? She has children. Having relatives who care and perhaps have jobs definitely increases a person's agency. She owns a home. That, in and of itself, may indicate she has some financial autonomy.

Let's consider Julia. She is Latina; she reads Spanish well but doesn't read English. She speaks English very well but still has a deep accent. Julia is transgender. She is very pretty and attracts attention everywhere she goes. She is in the United States with a green card, so she can work legally. However, her papers indicate that she is male. Julia is living with friends, but she wants to move out and get an apartment of her own.

Why is getting an apartment going to be difficult for Julia? Finding a job to support herself in the United States is going to be difficult for Julia because of two factors: her lack of literacy in English and the disparity between her gender appearance and her documentation. And let's face it, she's going to face racism, heterosexism, and transphobia. Many property managers discriminate against trans individuals.

The good news is that Julia has friends. She also could move to an area that is more trans friendly and more friendly to Latinas. For instance, Washington D.C. has laws that fight trans discrimination and resources to help Latinos get situated there. That will, by no means, pave the way for an easy life, but it might be a little easier. Julia has also demonstrated that she believes in herself and that she can make a better life for herself simply by moving to the United States.

Leslie is a sixteen-year-old who has left home and is couch surfing with friends. She is a junior in high school but not attending school much. She likes smoking marijuana and left her home because she was beaten by her mother, especially because of the marijuana. Leslie has her driver's license, although she doesn't have a car, and she is in possession of her social security card. But she hasn't been able to find a job. One or two of the parents where she's staying the night have offered to call Child and Family Services to see if she can get some longer-term help.

The biggest hardship that Leslie faces is her age. Many companies that used to hire minors have begun to only hire people who are eighteen and older. Finding a way to support herself (and her marijuana hobby) is going to be difficult. She will also find more difficulties if she doesn't finish high school. Plus there's that pesky hobby–marijuana. It leaves Leslie vulnerable to police and with a little less motivation to change her situation.

Leslie is lucky to have those couches to sleep. Clearly, she's got friends. Perhaps she's likable or pitiful. She inspires people to help her. She also must have some dedication since she's trying to stay in school. Leslie's age could also be of benefit to her. Since she's still a minor, the government may be able to step in to provide a safe home for her. There are those who wonder whether this is a good thing or a bad thing.

You might notice that I haven't said that any of these people are in sex work. But any one of them could be. Because finances are difficult and there are biases each of them face, sex work may be an option for them.

Because agency is a continuum, we have to treat each individual differently. But a good goal for everyone in sex work is to increase agency. The more agency we have, the more ability to face what comes our way, from illness to financial ruin. A person who has good agency is more likely to visit a doctor and seek treatment options when ill. A person with good agency is more likely to face financial issues straight on, working with bill collectors until everything is paid.

And the most wonderful thing about agency is the more you use it, the more you have!

# 3

# Pour Some Sugar on Me

## *Money*

Easy operator come a knockin' on my door

—DEF LEPPARD

Five years ago, after about two years of working full-time with Star Light, the nonprofit I founded, I was having limited success (meaning no success) at fundraising. My bills were bigger than I could imagine and the debt collectors were calling. I owed money on my student loans, the IRS, and utilities, and I was tapped out. There was no money in my account.

The IRS called and left a message.

I took a deep breath and called them back. A man answered the phone, and I gave him my social security number. I was behind on payments.

He asked why.

I said, "Because I'm a bad person." Financial worries can really change the way you feel about yourself.

"Reverend Scholl," the IRS agent said, "I am sure you are not a bad person. You are a person who is going through a tough time." Would you consider it sad to have your self-esteem restored by an IRS debt collector?

During that period of my life, if someone had asked me to have sex for money, I might have jumped at the chance. The number one motivator for individuals to get into sex work is money. The lack of money, whether real or perceived, is the root cause of sex work in all shapes and forms. No one would trade sex if there was no need for the prize, usually money, attached to it.

The 1998 winner of the Nobel Prize in Economics, Amartya Sen, believes that the distinguishing feature of poverty is the lack of freedom to have the ability to make meaningful choices that affect one's situation.[1] Sen is best known for recognizing that food shortages are caused not only by lack of food but also by unfair distribution.

It's important to recognize entering sex work isn't for lack of money but often because of the unfair distribution of wealth and influence in our societies.

Take the British divorcee who isn't getting enough in alimony to take care of the kids but doesn't have the education to go out and get a job. She rents a small apartment in a nearby borough and does incall appointments each afternoon while the kids are in school, combating both the loneliness of her new situation and the stigma of poverty ("going on the dole" in the United Kingdom).

Another example is the young college student who knows that she needs to go on to graduate school to achieve what she wants. She also knows, however, that her postgraduation salary won't pay back student loans. Sex work becomes a way to finance the dreams of her future.

Yet another case is the forty-eight-year-old Washington, D.C., resident who has sex occasionally with her ex-boyfriend so that he'll give her a little extra money so she can pay her light bill or get a few groceries.

Poverty is defined as the state of being extremely poor. But money concerns stretch across all financial and class lines. In a booming economy, everyone wants to make money. In a recessed or depressed economy, everyone needs to make money just to survive.

In the 1990s when I started Star Light, there were sex workers earning as much as midlevel managers. Even in small cities, I would talk with exotic dancers who were making over $100,000 a year. One dancer said to me, "What do you have to offer me? I make a lot more money than you do!" Some escorts report making as much as $4,000 in one night, while others say they earned between $2,000 and $3,000 a week.

The posteconomic meltdown may be a bit different. I hear young women saying that their clients are much more particular, much more demanding, and unwilling to lavish them with the same pay. It doesn't statistically bear out that more women are doing street-level sex work because of the economy, but there is some evidence that there are more Internet escorts due to the current economic climate. There are certainly more people who are unofficially trading sex for something they need—a little help with the rent, some groceries, maybe some drugs to take away the fear and the worry for just a little bit.

In 2010 at HIPS (Helping Individual Prostitutes Survive), when a new client would come in, we would walk them through an intake form. The purpose of the form was to identify the gaps in their financial life. Is there housing? Is there food? Is there clothing? Is there transportation to the important things they must attend? Many times people answered that those things weren't available. Housing might include sleeping on a friend's sofa or staying in an empty apartment. It may even be sleeping in a tent. Their food was what they could get from the local food bank or their food stamps allocation. Clothing was what they could carry in their bag. Transportation was a sporadic ride, depending on someone else to get to important meetings, including their health providers and support systems.

Money problems are like a nagging headache that won't go away. You can't pray it away. You certainly can't eat it away. You can't even laugh it away. Some days it may feel like an anvil crushing your head. Other days it feels like a tapping in the back corner of your skull. On the good days, it's just pressure behind your eyes. Poor people wonder how they're going to pay their rent or phone bill. Then they wonder how they're going to get transportation to their grandmother's house for Sunday dinner. Every out-of-the-ordinary expense sends them panicked, checking their accounts to see if there's enough money to cover what's needed and then checking when the next bill is due.

Take banking as an example. You know that nice little fee you get for having an account balance below $1,500? If you can't maintain that balance you'll pay about $12 a month in fees just for using the bank. That's $144 a year.

On the fifth of the month, the bank takes its $12, and this poor person forgets to enter it in her registry. Because of the oversight, she bounces a check, has to pay her bank to cover those charges, has to pay a surcharge (sometimes as much as $35), and finally needs to cover the fee the merchant will charge (another $35). So she just paid $70. If you make $8 an hour, that's more than a full day's wages. Unfortunately, when mistakes like this happen, they don't usually happen just once. It takes a few days to find out that a check bounced and by then, other checks have been written.

In an impoverished area, there are fewer fresh foods and more processed foods in grocery stores. One of the services HIPS offered in their urban center in Northeast, Washington, D.C., was daily lunch. We'd go to the grocery store weekly for healthy foods to feed our neighborhood friends–usually twelve to fourteen people who might not eat for the rest of the day.

When we first moved into the neighborhood, the chain grocery down the street had very little to offer in the way of fresh fruit, vegetables, and fresh meat. The prices were quite high, too. We all found that shopping in our home neighborhoods was less expensive and we had greater variety. Then urban renewal began to happen in the neighborhood (i.e., a new high-rise was being built) and grocery prices dropped and variety increased.

Since money makes the world go round, the people with money facing emergency expenses don't suffer as much. It's the wealthier neighborhoods whose electricity is restored sooner. Wealthier neighborhoods pay less for their goods and services because of buying power. They don't face job losses in their neighborhoods at the same level. If you have $5,000 in your checking account, how much notice do you take when you lose $100?

Lack of money affects choices. We know that schools are worse in neighborhoods without high property taxes. We know that transportation is much more difficult in poor neighborhoods (ever try to get a taxi in a rough neighborhood?). We know that predatory lending is more likely to occur in poorer neighborhoods. We know people pay more for gas in low-income communities.

According to the U.S. Census Bureau, there were 42.9 million people living in poverty in the United States in 2009.[2] Have you ever thought about how many people that is and what they face? It's not just the fear surrounding not being able to pay their bills; it also includes the discrimination they face day in and day out.

But the *really* poor? The really poor don't have checking accounts. They may not have to pay rent because they pay the person they're living with a few dollars each month. Or they may have to pay their rent by the week in a motel. They may just have to be at the homeless shelter each evening. Most shelters follow a rule that if a guest stays one night, they're permitted to stay the next. When people are really poor, they lose the ability to make their own decisions–when to go to bed, what to have for dinner, when to eat that same dinner. Poverty robs your options.

Extreme poverty and sex work are intimately related, and the cycle is vicious. An individual can't make the rent, so she decides to trade sex. The money is good, so things look a little better. Then she gets into a coercive relationship for protection. A portion of her pay goes to the pimp. Her job satisfaction goes down, and she begins to use drugs a little here and there to numb herself. Then she begins to use a little more. One day, she approaches the wrong person, an undercover police officer, who arrests her. After fines, lost wages, transportation costs, and court dates, the case can be adjudicated, but this sets her behind even further. It's time to trade more sex.

One of my most stunning moments working with people who trade sex was in a courtroom. Facing the judge was a fifty-five-year-old African American woman arrested for a sex act. She was well known to the judge, as she had been to court with other issues, perhaps drug- or mental health–related. For that case the woman decided to plead guilty, saying to the judge, "I just want to get it over with." The prosecutor read the evidence and the police officer's statement, then said, "The defendant approached the officer and offered a $10 sex act."

This judge, who had been very fair to other defendants, pondered the case for a moment and rejected the prosecuting attorney's request for forty-five days in prison, sentencing her to ninety instead.

*Ninety days* for trying to earn $10 with a sex act.

Leaving off the question of *why* for the moment, consider what happens during ninety days of jail. Who pays the bills, takes care of the kids, or keeps the housing situation stable? When women get out of jail and are left with even less than they had before, where do they go then? They go to a homeless shelter. They go from drug-free environments back onto the streets where the drugs are readily available.

The whole cycle starts again.

In 2009 the poverty rate was 14.3 percent. That's 43.6 million people in the United States, the largest number in the fifty-one years for which estimates have been published. For a single person under the age of sixty-five, that's an annual income of less than $11,161. In 2009 women who worked full-time made 77 percent of what men who work full-time made.[3]

It takes money to live. If you have no money, you get government aid. If that doesn't cover your basic needs, then what?

Of course, you don't have to be poor to choose sex work. Some women want to finance a dream. An escort I know sold sex throughout the Middle East and Europe simply to get to see those areas and to know how sex workers are treated there. Others have paid their way through college or graduate school through sex work. Financing your dreams through sex work is fraught with danger because often-times those dreams get shattered when people find out how you earned your money. I have heard many stories of young women paying their way through college and getting hired at their dream jobs, then getting fired because someone recognized them.

People in sex work learn to fear the "Where do I know you from?" conversation. Women who dance in strip clubs frequently run into customers from the club. Some dancers work out of town to keep this from happening. If an escort happens upon someone from her work, she is usually protected—chances are that the customer doesn't want to be identified, either. But the question usually occurs because of familiarity. When the client asks, "Where do I know you from?" the safest answer is, "I don't know! You don't look familiar." When the client finally remembers the truth, he is unlikely to follow after her.

In 2010 Melissa Petro, a schoolteacher with tenure in New York, was outed as a former sex worker. Well, technically, she outed herself by being an ally to sex workers and by writing about her time as an Internet escort. She wrote,

> I accepted money in exchange for sexual services I pro-
> vided to men…I was able to bill myself as exactly what
> I was at the time: a graduate student, bored and curious,
> sexually uninhibited, looking to make a little money while
> having a little fun.[4]

Ms. Petro paid her way through graduate school by performing sex acts on men she met through the Internet. She's said, over and over again, that she didn't like trading sex and that it was a brief period of time. She was forced to resign her duties in her New York school where she taught art.

Like the sex worker who must rebuild a life upon exiting jail, Ms. Petro had to rebuild. The irony is that Ms. Petro was writing in defense of people who trade sex to make their lives safer so they would have more choices. For outing herself, Ms. Petro lost her options. Clearly, selling sex affects your ability to earn a living later in life.

You might ask, if everything was equal, everyone had shelter, food, clothing, and jobs they loved, would people still sell sex? In all honesty, I believe they would. Some people sell sex because of sexual desire. Some people would sell sex to get one step further up the food chain. Some people would sell sex because they like it.

If everything was equal, though, the desperation around sex work would diminish. Sex workers would be less likely to trade sex in risky situations. They'd be less likely to ignore their inner voice that says, "Run!" when a client is violent. They'd be less likely to have sex without a condom and risk HIV/AIDS and sexually transmitted infections. They'd be less likely to get into coercive relationships with pimps and more likely to keep more of their earnings.

So lack of money and lack of options don't just drive individuals into sex work, they also contribute to the danger in sex work. Desperation is a continuum. The more discriminated against, the more a sex worker lacks money and options, and the more likely she is to face violence, disease, and even death.

# 4

# R-E-S-P-E-C-T

## *Poverty, Discrimination, and Mental Illness*

Find out what it means to me

—ARETHA FRANKLIN

Discrimination is the unfair and unjust treatment of people based on race, gender, sexual expression, class, and age. Oppression, the sustained state of discrimination, keeps individuals from getting jobs they deserve, homes they can afford, and services they need.

Racism is the belief that one race or another is superior or inferior. We're all familiar with the civil rights movement in the sixties, and so many of us are accustomed to believing that racism is no longer an issue. People of color have equal opportunities, right? Everyone has equal access to all places, equal access to good schools, and equal access to higher education, right?

Wrong.

In nearly any city in the United States, public schools in predominately African American areas are worse than the schools in white neighborhoods. If all the schools are bad, the white children are more likely to be in private schools. And even when school opportunities are available, parents in poverty miss those opportunities because of their own lack of education. Individuals who haven't been educated don't always value education.

Another indicator of racism in the United States is minority representation in our governing bodies. In 2008 African Americans made up 12.4 percent of the general population in the United States.

At the writing of this, Barack Obama is our first African American president. But there are only forty-two African American individuals serving in the House of Representatives. There are 435 members of this congressional body. That's fewer than 10 percent of our House of Representatives who are black. There are currently no African Americans in the Senate.[1]

African Americans are underrepresented in the United States government but overrepresented in our prison system. Forty percent of prisoners in the United States are black.[2] The rates of murder and violent crimes against African Americans are much higher than whites.

Something is clearly wrong.

What shall we credit for this disparity? And what are we willing to do to change it?

What is the solution to racism? If I knew this, I would be doing it. I don't know how to fix it, but I do know that it starts with me. It starts with believing, *truly* believing, that all people are of worth—that race doesn't determine value. From there, it branches out to fight the fear of those who are different.

Sexism says one biological sex is inherently better than another. Many people don't believe sexism still exists in the United States. However, numbers tell us a different reality. First, sexism exists in government representation. Women hold 17 percent of the positions in the House and Senate. Yet 50 percent of the population of the United States is female.

Second, sexism exists in the corporate world. There are only twelve *Fortune* 500 companies with women at the helm.[3] And although women make up a large portion of the work force and have many roles in management, the three most prevalent jobs are administrative assistants, nurses, and teachers.

Are you getting the picture here? Women are certainly in the work force. They have opportunities in political offices and opportunities in the highest echelons of corporations. There are opportunities but very few of them.

If opportunities at the top of the food chain are bleak, think about them at the bottom.

The United States recession of 2008 impacted women greatly. Women were 32 percent more likely to have been in a subprime mortgage, making higher payments at a higher interest rate.[4] During the recovery that started in 2009, men had a net gain of 805,000 jobs. Women had a net loss of 281,000 jobs. There is no doubt that the recession has adversely affected all working citizens, but women have carried a large portion of the losses.[5]

Mothers are the most economically vulnerable population. A report called "Women and Men: Living on the Edge" by the Institute for Women's Policy Research states, "single mothers clearly fare worse (during the recession) than married mothers: 16 percent of single mothers report going hungry at some time in the prior year because they could not afford to purchase food."[6] As primary caregivers to children, women see an even greater impact of sexism.

The worst form of discrimination results in violence. Statistically, one in six women in the United States has been a victim of rape or attempted rape.[7] According to RAINN (Rape, Abuse and Incest National Network), 15 percent of all those females sexually assaulted are under the age of twelve. RAINN goes on to report that "girls ages 16–19 are 4 times more likely than the general population to be victims of rape, attempted rape, or sexual assault."[8]

One of the most common beliefs about sex workers is that women go into that line of work because they were sexually molested. Is sexual molestation a precursor to entering the sex trade?

There are, without a doubt, a large number of women in the sex industry who have been sexually molested. But there are a large number of women who are not in the sex industry who have been sexually molested. According to RAINN, 17.7 million women are survivors of rape or attempted rape.[9] And every one of those women has responded to their sexual assault in a different way. Some have gone into sex work, surely. Some have fought to close the sex industry. Some have gone to college, others have not. Some have married men, some have not.

Sexual abuse is not a precursor to sex work. I have met plenty of individuals in the sex industry who were not sexually abused before they entered the industry. And I've known many survivors of sexual abuse who did not enter the sex industry.

There is one other type of discrimination that is rarely talked about. It is discrimination against people with mental illness.

Let me tell you the story of Jennifer. She's a middle-class white woman in her early twenties. She lives on a farm with her family in a rural part of California. And while her family makes some money though cattle ranching and housing horses, there's not enough money to send Jennifer to college.

She also has a back injury that keeps her off the horses and in chronic pain. Her chronic pain has led to depression, which she battles, on her good days, with antidepression medication prescribed by her physician. On her bad days, she battles it with vodka. Straight.

Jennifer has been hospitalized for depression and bipolar disorder several times.

Despite the mental illness, the back pain, and the bipolarity, Jennifer has an intense desire to make it on her own. She refuses to accept "charity," which would be everything from financial aid to Medicare. No student loans, no free drugs from her doctor, no going to the charity hospital.

She started working in the sex industry as an exotic dancer. She'd work at the club in the next town, so her parents wouldn't find out. If her back pain flared up to the point that she could not work, she would just call in sick. There was no penalty for missing a shift in this little club. Feel good? Work. Feel bad? No work.

The problem was that working on the pole (required in the club) was really tough on her back. So a good night at work would lead to a few days of pain. So she started working as a private dancer where she could dance in such a way that her back wouldn't hurt. The flexibility in her work schedule was greater, and she found that she made more money in tips. Plus, she ran fewer chances of running into someone her parents knew.

With a call from the agency manager, Jennifer would drive to a meeting place—either someone's home, a hotel room, or a frat house—to meet her customer. Once there, the expectations vary. She might be doing a dance for a single man or a group of guys. Jennifer could even make extra money by selling sexual acts. There are degrees of sex acts, much like degrees of difficulty in gymnastics. One type of sex act is valued more than another.

She could charge by the hour. If the client requested she stayed for longer periods of time, she could, but it would cost more.

There are certainly benefits to this line of work for Jennifer and the bills she needs to pay. If Jennifer decides to numb herself with alcohol or illicit drugs, very few clients mind. She also is safe from conflict with her coworkers, since she never sees any of them. The only work relationship she worries about is with her manager, who she only interacts with when dropping off or picking up money. Most transactions are handled over the phone, so Jennifer doesn't have to fake her way through feeling better.

On their Web site, the National Center on Workforce and Disability mentions some common myths about people with mental health issues. One myth is a "person with a mental illness should only work at low stress jobs that require no interpersonal contact." They combat the myth by noting that individual talents and weaknesses are different and that jobs require different skills. They continue, "Rather than broadly generalizing about personal barriers, it is best to help job seekers with mental illness understand their own capabilities and how those capabilities fit into a specific job match."[10] Sex work makes sense for individuals who have mental health issues because of the flexibility and limited interactions with people.

Here in the United States, where work is so important, we are losing some of what made employment possible for individuals with differing skills, abilities, and needs. Seth Godin, in *Linchpin: Are You Indispensable?*, explains that since the outset of the Industrial Revolution, corporations have been working to design job positions so that workers can be easily replaced and easily trained.[11] We are automatons.

But mental illness lessens productivity and causes lost time at work. Corporations are unlikely to retain employees with mental illness due to lost time and erratic behavior.

Brooke suffers from severe, chronic depression. Since I met her in 2005, she's tried to commit suicide at least seven times. These aren't "cries for help" attempts at suicide but real attempts. Slitting her wrists, tying ropes to hang herself, taking pills, she's done it all. Through good mental health care and the fact that she does not want to leave her daughter alone, she has become adept at knowing when to hightail it to the hospital. She says, "When the voice inside just keeps driving me to go jump off the top of the building, it's time to go to the emergency room."

Brooke wrote,

A couple of weeks ago, a dancer who I barely know tried to hang herself. The pain of imagining her not in the world was overwhelming to me. I cried, sobbed, for at least 24 hours. When I saw her at work about a week later, I was in the bathroom. I waited until we were the only 2 people left in there and I spoke to her. You see, she is absolutely gorgeous. Black hair, crystal blue eyes, thin, exotic, 19 years young. I told her this. I went on to tell her how she took me back to a place where I had been so many times before. That endless black hole at the bottom of the earth. Under the heavy blanket of despair, smothering the very life out of me. It would be better, I knew it would, if the pain could just stop. No other way. No one would miss me, or even notice I was gone.

You see, I was diagnosed with severe chronic depression several years ago. I have self-medicated with alcohol and about as much cocaine as you would see in Scarface. Anything to numb myself. When that didn't work, I tried overdosing several times with a plastic bag tied over my head, hanging myself, walking to a bridge to jump (only to be stopped by cops), slitting my wrists 50 times . . . DAMMIT!!!!! I just wouldn't or couldn't die!!! In between, I have tried anti-depressants and even ECT (electroconvulsive therapy) to make me not want to die. Finally, after 25 different medication trials, and 8 to 10 sessions of uni-lateral ECT, a light bulb went off in my brain. I wanted to live. I wanted to wake up in the morning. I wanted to have coffee. I wanted to read the paper. I wanted to get my nails done. I wanted to talk to people. Something finally worked after I had given up all hope of getting better!! I followed up with a therapist who agreed to see me after office hours for a very small fee. (God bless her!) And for the first time in about 5 years, I realized what it would have been like for other people if I had killed myself . . .

I would have left my daughter with infinite amounts of pain, sorrow, and blaming herself. My friends would have gone over and over in their heads if there was something they could have done to help. People who barely knew me would have cried, and wondered the same thing. I would have escaped my own pain by transferring it to so many others, leaving them to deal with the repercussions and finality of my death.

As I heard the DJ calling me to the stage, I finished telling her that although I barely knew her, it wrecked my world to think of her gone. I told her to please come to me or someone for help if she ever felt that way again. Tears in her eyes, she actually hugged and apologized to me for what she had put me through. I kissed her cheek and ran to the stage. Anybody who thinks God doesn't do some of the best work in strip clubs is sadly mistaken!!! You'll never guess what my DJ played to me to dance to . . .

There's nothing like a funeral to make you feel alive
(Quoted lyrics from Sixx AM,
"Life Is Beautiful")[12]

It is our job, as people who love people who work in the sex trade, to understand depression and mental illness so that we can provide alternatives to oppression.

We've established that women, especially minorities, are paid less and have fewer opportunities. They face a huge uphill battle for equality. Having fewer options because of gender is unfair and unjust. But this argument is predicated on the idea that gender is binary—there are only two genders, male and female. But binary gender does not clearly describe a lot of people's life and experience. The discrimination they face is even greater.

We now know that because of biological and hormonal differences, gender is a continuum. Male and female are not exact opposites; many males exhibit gender characteristics we consider to be feminine, and many females exhibit gender characteristics we consider to be masculine. Gender isn't an either/or proposition.

Any primer on sex, gender, and orientation has to begin with a few definitions. *Sex* is the designation determined by biological factors including reproductive organs, hormones, and secondary characteristics like facial hair and high voices. We are assigned a sex at birth, based on visible sex characteristics. We use the words male and female to denote them; there are only two designations.

*Gender* is defined as the cultural understanding of how biological sex plays out in the world; we use the words man, woman, boy, and girl to denote gender. This influences our beliefs on gender—for example, we expect women to wear lipstick and men to have short hair.

*Orientation* indicates the sex of the individuals to whom we're attracted. Three kinds of orientation are heterosexual, homosexual, and bisexual. We are born a sex, we live as a gender, and we feel attracted to individuals who are born a sex and live as a gender. That's our orientation.

It sounds simple, except it isn't.

Biological sex actually has a multitude of possibilities. Rather than just male or female, there is a continuum from male to female, and we all land somewhere on it. Studies indicate that at least one in five hundred individuals are born with visible male genitalia who find out later that they have a uterus and ovaries. Others have not only visible female anatomy but also higher male hormones and corresponding traits and orientation. How would you assign sex in these cases? There are other individuals who are born with both a vagina and a penis and testes. Which sex should we assign for them?

What about gender? First, what are the indicators? For women, is it high heel shoes, small feet, curvy hips, visible breasts, dresses or skirts, jewelry, high voices, long hair, makeup, manicured finger-nails, gentleness, being emotional, or subservience? How about the way we're social with one another?

Gender follows us throughout the choices we make in adult-hood. Traditionally, women have children, are primary caregivers to them, act more often in support roles in their jobs, do dishes, clean their houses, sew and make crafts, and watch chick flicks.

But for men, jocularity, physical prowess, athleticism, strength, courage, virility, short hair, pants, facial hair, and square jaws tell us "male." And let's not forget the Adam's apple! Men manage, are bosses, watch sports, drink beer, and are supposedly in control of their emotions at all times.

But gender isn't two poles. There are women who hate to wear dresses and skirts, who refuse high heels, who are bosses, who watch sports, and who aren't caregiving or interested in children. And some men like to socialize, sew, and cry at movies. There are men who are primary caregivers, who clean their houses, and make crafts. There are men who get manicures.

Gender is a continuum, too.

There are also people who are born one sex but feel like a dif-ferent gender. A child can be born with female genitalia but be masculine in her actions and mentally–both in feelings and in pro-cessing. And although society pronounces her female, she feels male.

People who feel their gender matches their sex at birth are called cisgender. People who feel their sex and gender do not match are called transgender.

Imagine feeling like a little girl but having everyone treat you as a little boy. You would never escape feeling different in some way, confused. That is why many transgender people take steps to appear on the outside as they feel on the inside. Medical interven-tions, including hormone therapies and surgery, can help individuals achieve the harmony that most are afforded at birth: to have their sex match their gender and to feel congruent.

If you had been born different and that difference caused you anxiety and psychological pain and you could change it, would you?

What if, instead of having male or female, men or women, straight or gay, we had varieties of sexes, varieties of genders, and varieties of orientations? What if we treated people as the unique, full spectrum individuals they are instead of requiring they fit into our predefined molds? What if we provided safe places for people to be themselves, wholly, divinely themselves?

There are individuals who are gender nonconforming whose attraction is not limited to one sex or another. They may call themselves "queer." The current use of the word queer began out of a reclamation movement. Queer was a slur against homosexuals. By reclaiming the word, it has a new meaning, and that word is infused with good connotations rather than bad. Most individuals who call themselves queer are saying that sex, gender, and orientation are not the criteria by which they live their lives, nor are they the criteria by which they choose partners.

Similarly, around 1 percent of individuals are born with an intersex condition, meaning they have characteristics of both male and female. The Intersex Society of North America says, "Intersex is a socially constructed category that reflects real biological variation."[13] Sex, gender, and even orientation are not as clear cut as we've been led to believe.

In fact, like all of nature, even in sex, diversity is the rule rather than the exception.

So how are we to respond to people who fall outside of that heteronormative structure society has imposed on people? There are those who believe people outside of the male-female binary should be reeducated to fit into society's structure. Some would recommend therapies, prayer meetings, and church services where "the gay is prayed away." Some would recommend exclusion from church and from society. Some would recommend freedom in feeling but not in action, suggesting that individuals remain celibate for life. At best, these responses are judgmental and do not work. At worst, they are precursors to violence.

I think about sex and gender, and indeed, all differences of race, status, and levels like this: God has given us a way to know ourselves best. It is in intimate relationships. Sure, you can know yourself outside of relationships—you discern your likes and dislikes, your appetites, your intellectual and spiritual boundaries. But it is through intimate relationships that we learn our emotional boundaries. We learn how we act in stress. We learn where we are selfish and where we are selfless. We learn where we are lovable and where we need some work. If we ask individuals to forsake intimate relationships, we are asking them to never fully know themselves, to never feel what it's like to be loved and what it's like to love. How could God, who is love, condemn a person to live without love?

There are other options. There's the option of acceptance. We can offer acceptance to people no matter what their differences, embrace the idea that we are all made differently; that none of us is exactly like the other; and that love is the source, the fabric, and the purpose of creation. And hence, love is the intention of the Creator.

When I was in my late twenties, I had been away from church for a long time. A friend from a former church told me about where he was attending. "There are gay people in our Sunday school," he said, "and we accept them for who they are!"

This alone convinced me to visit.

After attending for a few years, I asked a senior adult why she had chosen to attend this congregation. She answered, "The television show *60 Minutes* did a segment on homosexuality and said that it was likely genetic. I know that God don't make no junk, and I wanted to go to a church that honored this."

There are differing levels of acceptance and nonacceptance offered to gay, lesbian, bisexual, transgender, queer, and intersex people. There are people who picket funerals of known homosexuals with signs that read, "God Hates Fags," and the like. There are those who quietly discriminate. They don't speak out against nonconformists but instead avoid places where they might be confronted with such people. They don't employ anyone who might be gay or transgender.

I was at the hardware store recently and a transgender person had just gone through the line ahead of me. The cashier said to me, "There's a man in women's clothing over there. Some people!" I struggled with the appropriate thing to say. It's difficult to give a lesson in transgender acceptance when you're standing in a line at a hardware store. I did say, "You know we all have our things, don't we?" The cashier looked at me funny. But she understood that I was not standing with her in her ridicule.

In church circles, there are those who are welcoming but with an expectation that individuals will change if they attend church. A moderate pastor might say, "It's OK that people are gay, but it's not God's best plan." Some do get that the church is love, and there's no exclusion in love. If we believe God has a plan for every life, then we must believe everyone deserves to be a part of his plan. Who are we to say whether someone deserves to be accepted and embraced or not?

Acceptance is only the first step. Inclusion is good. Celebration is better. If we celebrate with our friends who come out, we are saying, "God didn't make any junk."

I met a lovely trans woman in Washington, D.C.. She was a Christian, and following her coming out as a woman, she wanted to be rebaptized as a sign of her new life and her new relationship with God and herself.

Her pastor agreed to baptize her, which sounds really great until the pastor insisted that she show him her newly remade genitalia. What was to be a wonderful sign of her new relationship with God as a new person, a person more fully herself, became a time for her to be abused by the clergy and a time to face gender harassment. What a welcome, right?

According to the recently released report titled *Injustice at Every Turn: A Report of the National Transgender Discrimination Survey*,[14] "Discrimination was pervasive throughout the entire sample [of 6,450 transgender and gender nonconforming individuals]." Statistically, trans and gender nonconforming individuals have double the rate of unemployment as gender normative individuals; 90 percent report harassment at work; 47 percent said they had been fired, not hired, or denied a promotion due to being trans or gender nonconforming; and 16 percent said they "had been compelled to work in the underground economy for income (such as doing sex work or selling drugs)."

While 16 percent may not seem huge, let me be clear. Of those who consider themselves transgender, female-to-male and male-to-female, one out of six have traded sex or sold drugs. The number goes up to one in five if when only talking about individuals who are transitioning from male to female (MTF). That's 20 percent of all trans women who have participated in an underground economy. But when you layer racism into the discussion? Forty-seven percent of African American transgender individuals have traded sex. Fifty-three percent have participated in underground economies.

Think about it like this: the most exaggerated figure ever given about the number of people trafficked in the world is 27 million. If we read the 2011 Trafficking in Persons Report, we see that one in nine trafficked individuals are in forced prostitution.[15] So 3 million (which is probably a very high estimate) are in sex slavery. Of our population, 27 million "slaves" would only be less than half 1 percent of the total population of the world. If it's just sex slaves, we're talking about less than half of one-tenth of a percent. But for trans individuals, it's 16 percent and for African American trans individuals, it's 47 percent.

A friend asked me once why it was so important to include so much information about transgender sex workers, because they are not the highest percentage of individuals in the sex trade. They matter because they are the most likely to enter sex work, most likely to be targeted by the police, and most vulnerable to violence. Police understand that if they meet a transgender woman of color, there's nearly a 50 percent chance that she's trading sex.[16]

Are you beginning to see how this type of discrimination can cycle out of control? So much so that a trans individual could find that sex work is a good option, perhaps the only option, for them? Difficulty in getting identification can lead to joblessness and homelessness, which leads to being on the street and vulnerable to police interference.

Not all the respondents to the survey were trans women (or individuals transitioning to female). Trans men (people transitioning from female to male) do not always face the same sort of discrimination, mainly because of two factors. First, it's not as obvious that a woman is transitioning to a man because of testosterone. Facial hair is a secondary sex characteristic that is nearly unmistakable, and taking testosterone shots brings facial hair. In other words, often times trans men "pass," or hide their transition, much easier. Second, trans men take on more privilege as they transition. In our culture, men have more power and influence, whether earned or unearned, and by transitioning from female to male, trans men gain power.

Trans women face nearly impossible odds at employment. They find jobs if, and really only if, they already had some privilege prior to transitioning–and that privilege diminishes after their transition.

Again, trans women of color fare far worse than their white counterpoints. Twenty-two percent of white trans folk indicate that they have been harassed by the police, compared to the 60 percent of African American individuals. Thirty-eight percent of African American trans individuals face housing discrimination, while only 15 percent of white trans individuals were discriminated against for housing. Do you see the intersections of oppression?

If you're transgender, it's hard to get proper identification, to find housing, and to find employment. Sex work becomes a real option because of these discriminations.

Sometimes people encounter more than one type of oppression, whether racism and sexism, transphobia and ageism, or homophobia and sexism. Scholars call this intersectionality. This means that more than one of these oppressions may affect you.

For instance, let me tell you about Jaqueé. Jaqueé is an African American trans woman from the South. She's tall, slender, and has a beautiful face and hair. She also has a very deep voice.

What are the intersections of oppression that Jaqueé has faced? First, she comes from poverty, which has in turn left her with an education level of fifth or sixth grade. She's very smart, but she cannot keep up in an office environment because she cannot write a good e-mail or a proposal. So she faces classism, in that she is not up to speed in our economy. She faces racism by the virtue of the color of her skin. But she faces sexism because she presents as female. And then, to top it off, she faces transphobia from people who don't understand being transgender.

So how does this work out in Jaqueé's life? Well, she has a really difficult time finding meaningful work. Or any work, for that matter. Then she has a difficult time with social services because her birth name and birth gender do not match her current gender. Because she is trans, she is more likely to be picked up on the street with the supposition that she is a "working girl." When she walks into a store, she is likely to be watched closely. One of the stigmas she faces, like all trans women and women of color, is the idea that she's also a thief. Jaqueé is also HIV positive. She has been refused housing because of transphobia.

Would you be able to keep a positive outlook?

There are multiple privileges that many of us have. Privilege is a special right, advantage, access, or immunity granted or available to a particular person or group of people based on arbitrary factors. Most people do not realize they have privileges. Privilege, in the human rights conversation, is usually unearned. Privilege can be based on race, gender, sexual orientation, age, and class.

A few months ago, a white male friend who is a pastor said, "I don't have any privilege. I shed it years ago." The reality of privilege is that it cannot be easily shed. People either have it or they don't, and while a person can gain some privileges (like education), it isn't easily shed. A white male may believe that he is not given more power by the people around him simply because of his skin color, but he is. By virtue of being a white male, he is ahead of his brothers who are African American or his sisters who are white. Unlike his African American brothers, he is probably not greeted with fear when he walks down the street. And unlike his white sisters, he probably does not feel the fear that women feel from male strangers on a dark street.

Most of us also face privilege and oppression at the same time. Take me, for instance. I have a lot of privileges. I am white. I have a graduate degree. I have connections in society. I am able-bodied; I am healthy and active. I am straight. I am gender conforming.

But I also face oppression. I already shared how, because I have chosen to work in religion, a male-dominated profession, I have been told, on multiple occasions, "You can't be a minister! You're a girl!" I have listened to professors spend two hours regaling the superiority of males by using the second chapter of Genesis, where Eve comes from Adam's rib. I have faced gender discrimination in the workplace (a liberal pastor of a church called me once and said, "You are the favorite and best candidate for the job, but we need to hire a man, for diversity sake"). I have seen and survived violence at the hands of a male. I am afraid sometimes when I walk alone at night.

In all honesty, though, I am much more privileged than oppressed. I have been afforded opportunities that I have not earned and do not deserve. That's the nature of privilege.

Privilege and oppression are not a zero-sum game. One person's privilege does not determine that another is oppressed. It's not that simple. We must recognize that all things are not equal, and we cannot live with the illusion that they are, especially not in the United States. Opportunity is not equal and we are not all able to pull ourselves up by our bootstraps.

Just because privilege and oppression make the world unequal does not mean that we walk away, willingly, from our privilege. Instead, it means that we use our privilege to make sure that other people have choices. We build choices for others, even while using our privilege.

When there are layer upon layer of discrimination, a woman's choices are limited. We use our privilege to build choices for women, including trans women, so that sex work isn't their only option and isn't even the best option.

# Section 2
## It's a Living: The Cycle of Sex Work

# Hadassah's Story

## *Such a Time as This*

My mother died in childbirth, and my father died of a broken heart. People still talk about my mother's beauty, her courage, and how much she loved my father. They were inseparable. Even in places that women were not allowed, my mother accompanied my father because they couldn't bear to be apart.

After my parents' deaths, my uncle Mordecai adopted me. He and his wife were childless, and they treated me as their own. From all accounts, their marriage was very different from that of my mother and father. Adina is gentle. Mordecai is gruff. Adina likes the home life. Mordecai likes the bustle of the streets. Adina likes cats, Mordecai only believes in farm animals. Although they love one another, they enjoy their time apart, their different interests, and a break from one another.

I never doubted Uncle Morty or Aunt Adina loved me. They gave me a full childhood with laughter and adventure, educating me in the ways of the home and in religion, even when many girls don't get that kind of education. Uncle Morty taught me to read and write. Aunt Adina taught me to cook.

A few weeks after my twelfth birthday, news came from the city that the king had expelled his wife, Vashti, from the palace. They say that she disobeyed a direct order from the king. Vashti was beautiful and beloved, and the people all thought that the king was impudent and imprudent in putting her out. The announcement was made that the king was looking for a new queen.

Uncle Morty and Aunt Adina sat me down that afternoon. After telling me the story of my mother and father, how my mother was so beautiful and loving, how she and my father loved each other so deeply, Uncle Morty said to me, "You are as beautiful as she was. And as genuine and loving. I believe you would have the opportunity to be queen."

Queen? Me? But I was just a child. And the king clearly wasn't looking for a wife to love but a wife who would obey.

I didn't believe my uncle Morty. While others had always told me that I'm beautiful, I think I look strange. I have bright blue eyes, while those around me have brown eyes. My skin is pale, unlike my loved ones, who have dark skin. I'm bony, skinny, and have knobby knees. My breasts are small and my fingers seem extraordinarily long. I don't believe Uncle Morty's assessment.

But it is the life of an orphan to obey.

Uncle Mordecai and Aunt Adina had different ways to prepare me for going to the king's palace. Uncle Mordecai sat with me for three days teaching me the history of the Jews. "You are a Jew," he said, "and you must always remember that, even as you must never reveal it." I learned about the creation, Adam and Eve, the family of Abraham and Sarah, Moses and wandering in the desert, and Judges and Ruth. I learned that the Jews have a rich tradition of strong women. I learned that we were part of the diaspora of Jews away from our temple but still a people who cared for one another and served our God. I learned ways to worship the Lord without having a community around me.

I also learned that gentiles haven't always been good to the Jews. Moses lived in Egypt, was raised by the pharaoh's family, and left only after watching an Egyptian soldier kill a Jew with no consequences. I heard about the pharaoh's refusal to let the Jews go and the plagues that followed. I learned about the strength of the Hebrew people as they left Egypt, the land of their security, when God called Moses to lead them out.

From Aunt Adina I learned about pleasing a man. She laughingly taught me some tips in flirting, how to bat my eyes and toss my hair. She also taught me how Persian women wear their hair uncovered, how they dance for the pleasure of men, and how they differed from Jewish women. She helped me become a little less like a child. She also helped me choose an Persian name. My parents named me Hadassah, but I chose Esther for myself, because Esther means star.

From both Adina and Mordecai, I felt the full measure of my Jewish roots and the joy and pleasure that could come from the Egyptian culture.

Uncle Mordecai accompanied me to the palace, where we were met by Hegai, the wonderfully flamboyant watch guard of the harem. As is tradition, I brought Hegai some sweets that I had made for him, little triangular fruit-filled cookies. By his large size, it was obvious that he like treats, and he exclaimed that they were perfection on a plate! He also exclaimed over my beauty and put me in a special place in the harem.

For over a year, I spent time in the harem, getting beauty treatments and learning queenly ways. I sat with Hegai often as he told me the stories of the royals and let me see the intrigue of the palace from a different point of view.

I also spent time getting to know the other women in the king's harem. There were women from all over Persia. Because Egypt was a wealthy kingdom, there were women from all over the world, beautiful women who gave up lives with their families for the chance to be a queen.

During this time, I also studied the laws and mores of this kingdom. I learned the customs of royalty, when it was appropriate to speak to the king and when it was appropriate to be quiet. I learned how to eat with other kings and queens. I learned the habits of a queen.

But I was not the queen, and the king did not ask for me.

Then my turn came. I would be granted one item to take with me, and I would go see the king in the afternoon and spend the night with him. We would lie together. On the following day, I would move away from the virgins to another part of the harem. I would not get another chance with the king unless I found favor with him and he asked for me. I asked Hegai, "What should I bring?"

"My child," Hegai answered, "take those cookies to the king. They are heavenly cookies, and the king loves a treat. I'll make a way for you to use the kitchens, and your beauty and your cookies will make you stand out." I did as Hegai suggested.

I went to see King Xerxes. He greeted me in his chambers with a piece of jewelry and a speech about how grateful he was that I would come to his harem and serve him in this way. I bowed my head. I tossed my hair. I presented the cookies.

Suddenly, Xerxes' face changed. He smiled at me and pulled me to him. "Tell me, Esther," he said, "tell me about yourself."

He poured a glass of wine for me.

I asked the king, "Please, my lord and king, tell me about yourself."

Xerxes told me about his life, about his mother and grandmother. He told me how difficult it is to be the king and yet how grateful he is for the chance. He told me how beautiful I was.

We were together that night.

In the morning, the king pulled me to him again. "You are the one," he said.

I didn't return to the harem. I was shown to a beautiful chamber that rivaled the king's chamber. I had a new household of people. There was a large party, and the king placed a crown upon my head. And jewelry! Oh, the jewelry! I asked if Hegai could come see me.

"My queen?" he asked when he came in. "You called for me?"

I begged Hegai to call me Esther. "I will call you Queen Esther," he said, "but protocol requires that I call you queen."

"I need you to teach me that protocol," I said to him.

He replied, "I serve at your pleasure, my queen."

After all the fanfare, my uncle Mordecai remained at the king's gate. He really loved to know what was going on in the community and he worried about me. While he was there, he uncovered a plot to kill the king. He told the king's men and saved the king's life. The king promised to do something good for the House of Mordecai.

After several years, the routine became normal. I lived in my lovely quarters, and I tended to the king's household needs. One afternoon, Hegai came to me. "Your uncle is outside," he said, "wishing to speak with you." Because I couldn't leave the palace without the king's permission, I sent another eunuch from the king's service to speak with my uncle.

The king's second-in-command, Haman, was plotting to kill all the Jews present in Persia. Mordecai, who distrusted Haman from the beginning, told the king's eunuch and expected me to tell the king. It had been several weeks since the king had called for me, and I couldn't just go to the king without being called. I told Uncle Mordecai that I couldn't tell the king.

"Don't think that because you are in the king's house, you will be exempt from this violence. If you remain silent at this time, relief and deliverance for the Jews will arise from another place, but you and your father's family will perish. Who knows but that you have come to your position for such a time as this?" Morty exclaimed.

But I didn't trust myself to go see the king. I didn't trust that I could say the right things. I didn't trust that I wouldn't get myself killed. I didn't trust that I was powerful enough to convince the king. Any person who approached the king was subject to be killed unless the king extended his scepter.

But the words of Uncle Morty rang in my head. "Who knows but that you have come to the kingdom for such a time as this?"

For such a time as this . . . I sent word to Uncle Morty to gather the people together to pray. I was going in.

I wore my finest jewels, styled my hair, and put on perfume. I went to see the king. When I walked into the room, his face lit up, and he extended his scepter to me. He asked, "What can I do for you, my queen? Up to half of the kingdom is yours."

I requested the king and Haman's presence at a banquet set for them. And while I didn't cook the entire dinner, I did cook the little fruit-filled cookies that the king liked so much. The king asked, "What would you like, my queen?" My only answer was, "Come to a dinner tomorrow with Haman. I will make my request then."

The king awoke late that night and pulled out some light reading to help him go back to sleep. He read the record of his reign. In that record he was reminded that Mordecai had saved his life. In the morning he asked his servants, "What good thing has been done for the House of Mordecai, who saved my life?" Nothing had been done.

Haman entered the king's courts. The king asked him, "How would you suggest I honor a man who deserves my honor?" Haman, being the likable fellow he was, assumed the king was talking about him, so he answered, "Give him a royal robe the king has worn and a majestic horse the king has ridden, one with a royal crest placed on its head. Lead him through the streets, saying 'This is how the king shows his honor!'"

The king said to Haman, "Let it be as you say. The man is Mordecai." Haman was seething at that point. He thought the king was going to honor him!

I awoke the next morning and they were erecting the gallows, intending to hang someone from them. I prepared the feast for the evening. The king and Haman joined me, and the king asked again, "What is your request? Up to half of my kingdom is yours."

When I answered, I told him of the plot to kill me and my people, that Haman had sold the lives of the Jews and was planning a massacre.

The king was so angry, he stormed out the door.

Haman stayed behind. He was so scared, he was shaking. He begged me, "Don't tell the king any more of this, and I will not call for the death of the people." I refused his offer, not looking at him. Then he began to come at me with some force. He pushed himself on top of me and slurred his words, saying that he would "show me a real man."

The king entered just at that moment, pulled Haman off of me, and ordered him hanged on the gallows. The king removed his signet ring from the finger of Haman and gave it to Uncle Mordecai. I made sure that Mordecai was appointed to lead Haman's estate.

Because Haman had ordered the Jews' deaths with the signet ring of the king, it could not be undone. The plan was in place to kill all the Jews. But the king offered Mordecai and me the ability to make a new decree and sign it with the signet ring. The new decree allowed the Jews to gather together, to defend themselves, and to seize the property of the people who attacked them.

My people rejoiced the end of Haman's power. They celebrated with feasts. People around them, people from other nationalities, became Jews because of the respect they had for them.

*       *       *

In modern times, Hadassah—or Esther, as she became known as—might be called sexually exploited. Her uncle Mordecai and aunt Adina, loving as they may have been, might be charged with trafficking in persons. Given how young she probably was, they might also be charged with endangering the life of a minor. The king would have his picture in the paper for paying for sex (being a John). Esther would have been taken from the palace and placed in a shelter with other youths.

Esther exemplifies the role of agency in the life of a sex worker. And yes, I called Esther a sex worker. She has an uncle who physically takes her to the king's residence (does that make her trafficked?). She is selected because of her beauty and consigned to have sex with King Xerxes. In return for having sex with the king, Esther is housed and fed. She has sex with him in the hopes that she will gain wealth and power.

How much say does Esther have in the whole process? Does she want to be in the harem? Does she want to have sex with the king?

Over and over again, we see Esther handing her decisions over to other people. Mordecai convinces her to join the harem. Hegai assigns her attendants and orders beauty treatments for her. Mordecai insists that she not tell people she's Jewish. Hegai chooses the clothes she wears in to see the king. The king chose Esther. Throughout the story, however, we hear nothing of her own wants.

There are factors that determine just how much choice Esther has in this story. Her age is a factor. She's very young, probably just in her teens, when this whole process begins. And she is at the mercy of her uncle, Mordecai. He has fed, clothed, and educated her, "adopted her as his own daughter" (Esther 2:7) and given her a home. Other factors that diminish her agency include her education level, her gender, and her race. Her people are not free in Persia. They are exiles from their own land.

But she has factors that increase her agency, too. She has people who care about her, her uncle Mordecai and aunt Adina. And because Mordecai is able to both get Esther into the harem and save the king's life, he has some sort of access to the palace. Most of all, she's beautiful.

We have to admit that Esther uses sex to get something that she needs. She uses her femininity and her sexuality to catch the king's interest, so much so that he marries her and makes her queen.

Esther doesn't seem to know that she has some power nor does she care to use it until one day when her uncle Mordecai comes to urge her.

Then she uses her sexual favor with the king to save her people. It's not just sex as a physical act, which is important, but it's also sex as power. Esther uses that power to convince her husband to do the right thing by the Jews.

Is it the threat of death that makes Esther take some action? Or is it just the acknowledgment that she can do something? Is it knowing that she has the power to change her circumstances and the circumstances of those around her that makes her act? I believe the biggest contributing factor for Esther was the belief that she could affect change.

Esther transforms her life, and she transforms the life of the Jews around her. She recognizes her own power, and she takes steps to use that power. She's also probably surprised at the depth of the love that people have shared with her over the years. After she wakes up to "such a time as this" (Esther 4:14), she sees that the king really cares for her (offering her the scepter is a big deal) and her uncle Mordecai needs her and believes in her, and so she saves her people.

Not bad for a couple of days' work.

# 5

# You Shook Me All Night Long

## *It's Just Sex*

Knockin' me out with those American thighs

–AC/DC

One of the biggest obstacles to understanding the sex industry and feeling compassion for the individuals who participate in the sex trade is that we must understand our biases about sex. Even more than that, we must overcome our discomfort so that we can understand other people's experience. In other words, we have to grow up about sex.

The urge often comes for me to stick my fingers in my ears when I hear about someone else's sexual preferences and what they like to do in the privacy (or not so private spaces) of a relationship. But trying to ignore someone or avoid hearing about something gives the impression of judgment. It's just not an effective way to build trust in a relationship.

If you make friends in the industry, you will hear stories of BDSM (bondage, domination, sadism, and masochism). You will hear stories of public sex, anal sex, oral sex, gay sex, straight sex, partnered sex, solo sex, and multipartnered sex.

You know what? It's just sex!

One early evening I was having dinner with a friend who is a professional dominatrix. Having never had many conversations about domme work, I took the opportunity to ask her questions to understand the work better.

"What are some of the things you would do on a date?" I asked.

"Well, we'll do a lot of domination talk. Or rather," she said, "I'll do a lot of talk. I tell them to shut up a lot. Then we move into the more sexual aspects of it. We may do CBT."

"CBT?" I asked.

"Cock and ball torture. I will apply pressure of some sort to his genitalia."

I cringed. Yes, I admit it. I cringed.

I damaged our friendship with that cringe, and that damage took months to overcome. The cringe wasn't about the work that my friend was doing; the cringe was about my own discomfort with the combination of sex and violence.

I maintain that working in the sex industry isn't about sex, but it does require (in most cases) sex. Knowing someone in the industry requires that we know something about sex, that we are comfortable talking about sex, and that we are open and accepting about people's sex preferences and styles—because not everybody does it missionary style.

There are all kinds of sex in the world. You may only like plain, old, vanilla sex. But there's chocolate, strawberry, peanut butter, mango, and bacon out there, too. And our sexuality says a lot about how we are in the world, how we are in relationships, how we love, how we enjoy pleasure, how we share intimacy. Sex is our flavor, and everyone has a different flavor.

In some ways this may mean revisiting all the things you were taught about sex as a child. Were you taught that sex was bad? Were you taught that it was a necessary evil? Were you taught that it wasn't important? Or conversely, were you taught it was good but only in one or two contexts? Were you taught that it's just OK?

Then check out the biblical record. Stories about sexuality abound. There's Adam and Eve realizing that they're naked. Does this mean that before the fall there wasn't a distinction between sex and not sex? Then there's Abram and Sarai—having sex at eighty-plus years of age! David and Solomon have sex, apparently with a lot of women. Song of Solomon is all about a young couple in love, unmarried and having sex. The book of Hosea, at its basest level, is the story of an open marriage. Hosea married Gomer knowing that she was a "promiscuous" woman (Hosea 1:2–3).

And even when confronted with an "adulterous" woman, Jesus, given the choice of throwing stones at her or offering her grace, offered grace.

If you've never unpacked your feelings and thoughts about sex before, I suggest you take a little time to do so. Here are some questions you may want to ask yourself:

- What did my parents teach me about sex, about the mechanics and emotions of it?
- What was my first sexual experience? How did it feel to me, both emotionally and physically?
- Was there ever a time when I engaged in sex that I didn't want? What were the circumstances surrounding that? Was it someone I knew or someone I didn't know? How did I feel, both emotionally and physically, afterward?
- What part does sex play in a relationship?
- What are my limits when it comes to the acting out of my sexuality? It is normal to have an "ick" reaction to some kinds of sex. All of us have limits. It's important to keep that reaction to yourself, though, if you're speaking with a sex worker.
- Are there any things in sex that I would like to try, fantasies that I have that I may or may not have acted out? How do these make me feel? Have I told my partner, and, if I have, would I like to try them?

Every person will have different answers to these questions. And these answers (and so many more) add up to your unique sexuality. There may not be anyone else in the world who has the same sexual feelings that you do. Even your partner may not have the same feelings and desires that you have.

There are also individuals who feel that they cannot have sex any other way than paying for it. Some of them, without a monetary contract, are turned down for sex all the time. There are also individuals who can have sex nearly any time they want it–they may be in relationships and may be sexually active with consenting partners who desire sex. These individuals still pay for sex.

And there are those individuals who say that they pay for sex not for the release of sexual activity or because they want to have more sex but for the absence of relationship, for the absence of judgment, and for the lack of emotional entanglement. They have sex for the rush of secrecy.

Many of the individuals I have worked with believe that their form of sexuality, whether paid or unpaid, is their right. Now that's a different thing altogether. They do not believe in nonconsensual sex, but they feel that anything goes with consenting adults.

This is a very important distinction when it comes to sexuality and understanding our "rights." Is it your right, whether you want to be submissive in the bedroom or you want to hit or be hit, to do as you please? There are so many different types of sexual attraction and sexual expression that do not fit in our typical view of sex.

What types of sexual relationships are there? Well, there are individuals who are nonmonogamous, who have multiple relationships with multiple people. These are also known as "open marriages." And while it may not be your ideal relationship, it works for many people. There are individuals who enjoy BDSM. In BDSM, there is usually a dominant and submissive partner. And while this can take many forms in the bedroom (being tied up, spanked, bruised on purpose), it can also be expressed in the relationship—the dominant personality may demand submission in decision making or domestic relations.

Individuals who like these alternative sexualities are attracted to sex work, both as consumers and as workers. They find it to be a safe and interesting way to live out their fantasies without being judged.

No one can tell you what your limits are, but there are some limits that should always be in place—or at least one limit. Sex must always be consensual. That means that both (or all) partners in sex must be able to consent, and consent must be given. No one is expecting you to get a consent form filled out in triplicate, but an honest conversation about what this sex act will mean to you and to your relationship is important at the beginning of any sexual encounter.

I have long maintained that if a couple cannot talk about sex, they probably shouldn't be having sex. Sex has the power to make relationships better, but it also has the power to make relationships worse. Even more than that, sex has the power to destroy people.

Imagine for a moment a woman who says, "I love sex!" What do you think of her? Do you assume she's had a lot of partners? Do you assume she's promiscuous? Do you think she is likely to participate in risky behaviors? Do you think she might drink, smoke, or do drugs?

Now imagine a man who says, "I love sex!" What characteristics do you picture? Can you imagine a monogamous man saying this? Sure you can. Can you also imagine a guy who has many partners?

Do you feel more judgmental toward one of these examples?

In many societies, including Western society, women are judged for being sexual, and men are affirmed for their prowess. Even if women's sexual needs do not exceed those of men, they are presented as sluts, whores, or trashy women. And while women who enjoy sex are portrayed as sluts, men who enjoy sex are called "players."

Many of the individuals whom I've met who were in sex work have expressed their reason for working in the industry this way: "I love sex. And since I love it and am good at it, I figure, 'What the heck? I'll make a living at it.'"

Our society is still stuck with the idea that women and men have different sexual needs, namely, that men want sex more than women do. And women who own up to their own sexual desires (especially if that desire is more sex, not more cuddling) are threatening, freakish, and somehow just not right. Why is behavior for one gender accepted and even commended while the same behavior for another gender is vilified and denigrated?

The assumption of promiscuity is also a determining factor in sex work. At a very young age, some girls are stereotyped around sex, called sluts before entering into their own sexuality. Even if they have not been promiscuous, they become sexually active, internalizing the expectations around them. This is significant. It means girls are living out the cultural presumption being thrust upon them. With many of the young women I've worked with, it's not so much "I love sex, I'll make a living at it" but instead "Everyone thinks I'm having sex anyway, so I might as well."

Women with multiple partners are still looked down upon in our society. Women are still valued more if they are virgins. Take, for instance, the books that have the expectation that young women will "save themselves" for marriage. There's *Sexless in the City* by Anna Broadway and *Real Sex: The Naked Truth about Chastity* by Lauren Winner. There is abstinence-only education in our schools that teach our kids that abstinence is the only way to avoid STIs (sexually transmitted infections), including HIV. We ask our daughters to make virginity pledges, often times to their fathers, as the only option.

When we value virginity and purity over anything else, we set up a value system that is unfair, especially when we do not hold men to the same standard. Men are expected to have multiple partners before marriage. Men are glorified for their sexual prowess, and women are vilified for having desires.

It's the old "Madonna versus Whore" syndrome. A man wants a woman who is willing to meet his sexual desires, but he wants her to be sexually pure. Men want either Jesus' mother Mary, who was a virgin even after having given birth, or Mary Magdalene, who is (perhaps wrongly)[1] credited to have been a prostitute. Or they want a woman who can be both at the same time. Do you see the impossibility of that?

In our society today, women are more open about their sexuality. The creation of *Girls Gone Wild* has brought about a more public sexuality where young women take their shirts off in front of the camera. Although these young women were often drunk, they signed releases and posed for the cameras topless or kissed other women. It's not unusual to see young women posting Facebook pictures depicting them making out with other women. Women are being more open about their desires.

Is this a good thing or a bad thing for women? Just like the question about whether sex work is good or bad, I think the question is loaded in the wrong direction. It just is. There are good things about it—it is good for women to be in control of their own sexuality. But there are bad things about it, too. Just like social media, being completely open about your sexuality at a young age can have ramifications that go beyond what you imagine. It seems as if many of the decisions being aired about sexuality are experimentation, and broadcasting your experiments seems premature.

I'm not in favor of taking our sexuality out of the public realm. In some way, the expression of sexuality has brought us to a more inclusive society. On the other hand, I think it should be thoughtful. Thoughtful sexuality will be nuanced, not black or white but shades of gray.

The biggest danger for women who express their sexuality is the judgment that comes from it. Employers, future spouses (and mothers-in-law), and men who oppose this expression are the difficulty. People are appraised by the messages they send. If we can stop doing this and especially quit holding women to a different standard than we hold men, then the world would be a safer place to explore women's sexuality.

Is sex a human right? Every body is made to experience sex, although many people choose not to and still others feel no imperative to have it. Audacia Ray, author of *Naked on the Internet*, said, "Sexual pleasure is a human right. Sex, the act/partnered sex, not necessarily." The reason partnered sex may not be a right can be summed up in one word: consent. In other words, it takes at least two consents for partnered sex.

Consent seems like it would be a cut and dry issue. Both people say "Yes!" and sex ensues. Rarely do partners say, "Would you like to have sex?" and wait for an answer. Instead, there may be implied consent, where consent isn't explicit but can be inferred from a person's actions. There can be nonverbal consent. There can also be consent that is not really consent, especially in the cases of coercion and force. A woman may be too afraid to say no to sex or she may be lied to in order to consent.

In addition to all that, there are factors that must be in place in order for a person to be able to consent.

In most states, age is a huge factor in consent. Although the laws vary, the assumption is that young people cannot consent to sex because they may not understand the full ramifications. Sobriety is a factor. There is a point in drug and alcohol use where you are unable to understand the full ramifications of your consent. Mental retardation, health issues, and mental health issues can all affect a person's ability to consent.

Consent is always important in sex. But what about in sex work?

There are a lot of people who believe that people engaged in sex work cannot exercise consent. From feminists who say that the patriarchy has infiltrated the sex worker's brain so deeply that she can't say "No" to the profamily groups who say it's spiritual darkness that leads women into sex work, people are always trying to say that women can't actually consent.

Melissa Farley of the End Demand movement, in an article titled "Prostitution and the Invisibility of Harm," writes,

> To assume that there is consent in the case of prostitution, is to disappear its harm. Social and legal assertion that there is consent involved in women's oppression is not new. Rape law, for example, commonly inquires whether or not the woman consented to any sexual act, rather than asking if the rapist obtained her freely given affirmative permission without verbal or physical coercion.[2]

Again, proponents of a black and white view of sex work are usually not nuanced enough. Independent escorts surely have the ability to say yes or no to sex. Some sex workers who have pimps or managers have the ability to say yes or no to sex. In fact, some managers protect the sex workers who work for them by making sure they have the ability to say yes or no. One of the main jobs of management in the brothel system in Nevada is to protect the consent of the workers in their establishment.

Are there others who have lost their ability and the freedom to say yes or no? Of course there are. It is our job as Christians and humanitarians to protect that freedom. But we cannot assume that a woman has lost her ability to say yes or no unless she says she had no choice.

There's a difference between the act of sex and the power of sex. There is a lot of power that goes along with the physical act of sex.

Just after college I worked at the Alabama Democratic Party hoping to understand the political process, how to include women more, and how to bring more progress to Washington and Alabama. It was my perception that the Democratic Party was working against racism and sexism in Alabama, so I was committed to the cause.

At my first high-priced fundraiser, I met a woman and we spoke for a while. She asked about my interest in politics, and I'm sure I spouted off an innocent statement about helping the poor and making sure that the government looked after the "least of these." She asked if I wanted to be a politician.

"Maybe I'd like to run political campaigns," I naïvely said.

She answered, "There's only two kinds of women in politics. Bitches and whores. Which will you be?"

*That's my option?* I thought. *I have to choose between the two?*

In other words, there are two ways for women to achieve power in the structure in which we live. We can dominate men (bitch) or have sex with powerful ones (whore). At my age, I didn't understand that there was a third way, a way that involved neither, that could build power as partnership and power through cooperation.

At twenty-two years old, I opted for neither. Not understanding other ways of building community and engagement, I sort of "stood down." I didn't want power through sex nor did I want it through force.

There is great power in the ability to offer sex or withhold it.

The ancient Greek play *Lysistrata* by Aristophanes is one of the first examples of the power of women's sexuality. The women decide to withhold sex until the men declare a ceasefire in the Peloponnesian War. When the men begin to walk around with painful erections all the time, they finally end the war.

In the summer of 2011, Vagisil aired a new commercial called "Hail to the V." This commercial features a woman cradling a baby in the moonlight, Cleopatra ruling over her subjects, two ninjas fighting over a Japanese maiden, and knights jousting for a princess. The voiceover says, "Over the ages, and throughout the world, men have fought for it, even died for it. One might say it's the most powerful thing on earth." Meaning that the way women get power is through the vagina.

Women can gain power by being involved with men, especially powerful men. A powerful man can be a shield against bad things, whether physical or financial, and seducing a man is one way to get his protection. Marrying power and wealth is another way. There are fourteen female, self-made billionaires in the world, as opposed to 665 male, self-made billionaires. Of the fourteen females, five of them started businesses with their husbands or brothers.[3] Only 20 percent of the businesses worth $1 million are owned by women. To be clear, nearly half of all millionaires are women, but most of them gained their money through birth or marriage.

Performing sex work can certainly heighten a woman's power not only financially but also through powerful men. Ashley Dupré traded sex with Eliot Spitzer, then-governor of New York. Following the exposé of their sexual relationship, Spitzer resigned. Ashley Alexandra Dupré, on the other hand, posed for *Playboy*, got a recording contract, and writes an advice column for the *New York Post*.

If sex is a way that women can achieve power, then how can we deny them that path? True, it may not be an ideal way to gain influence and power, but it's a valid way. However, women who gain their power through sex work face huge risks—they risk violence, shame, loss of reputation, and ostracism. Ashley Dupré gained power. Many do not.

It's the inequality between men and women that is most unfair. Yes, these inequities are the world we live in. But until we decide that we will not live with these inequities, which are also iniquity, nothing will change. If we hold one set of people accountable for their actions, we have to hold the other set of people accountable for their actions. Or if we overlook responsibility for one group, we have to release the other of responsibility, too.

Sex work is built on inequality. By recognizing this inequality and understanding the ins and outs of sex work, perhaps we can address the underlying causes. Maybe women will have more choices, and those who do decide to trade sex can be safer.

# 6

## Crazy Train

### Customers and the Cycle of Sex Work

I'm living with something that just isn't fair
—OZZY OSBOURNE

I received an e-mail from a friend telling me the story of her marriage. She explained that her spouse had seen sex workers during his first marriage. She insisted, however, that he wasn't still seeing sex workers in their marriage. "Our sex life was very good," she explained.

Because certainly, if they had a good sex life, he wouldn't want to visit sex workers (or look at porn, go to strip clubs, or call a sex line), right? And isn't the fact that they have a good sex life an indicator that he's not paying for sex?

In reality, he was paying for sex.

Ask a few people who trade sex about their customers and you're likely to get lots of different responses. Some of them have real affection for their customers. Some have had terrible experiences of violence with their customers. Some have been harassed by their clients through the Internet, on the phone, and in person. Some have had all those experiences.

There are a few terms used for individuals who pay for sex. One of my favorites is *punter*. The *Urban Dictionary* defines *punter* as "London slang for customer, may also be used for 'johns' (among prostitutes and police agents), people who watch porn movies or go to strip joints regularly."[1] In the United States, people who see escorts often are called *hobbyists*. According to Amanda Hess in the *Washington City Paper*, "They see themselves as connoisseurs, 'hobbyists'–artists, even. They see paying for sex as a sport which can be won by frequenting the most and best sex workers for the least amount of money, hassle, and consequences."[2] Punters and hobbyists are individuals who visit sex workers regularly, even as a sport.

And what are hobbyists looking for? Alex Johnson from MSNBC.com says,

> What they want is generally very clear: They want a center-fold model who will hang adoringly on their every word in public, then perform any sex act in any position with professional skill in private.[3]

The message boards of hobbyists give explicit details about what a specific "date" or sex worker will be willing to provide and usually rates the experience. For Internet escorts these ratings are very important and can make or break business.

Characterizing the types of men who visit sex workers is a futile effort. No two people pay for sexual contact and content for the same reason. Some are looking for sexual satisfaction. Some are looking for companionship. Some are looking for acceptance. Some are into the risk; others are into the comfort of seeing the same person over and over. There are no overarching types of individuals who visit sex workers. Nor are there any hard and fast rules about what kind of sex workers these men seek out. Some customers only like one type of sex work, whether it is porn, escorts, cam girls, phone sex, or exotic dancers. Strip club clients may not like porn. Porn viewers may not want to see escorts.

However, staunch antiprostitution activists will certainly try to characterize them. Melissa Farley, Emily Schuckman, Jacqueline M. Golding, Kristen Houser, Laura Jarrett, Peter Qualliotine, and Michele Decker interviewed 100 individuals who had purchased sex and 101 who had not. They compiled their findings in "Comparing Sex Buyers with Men Who Don't Buy Sex: 'You can have a good time with the servitude' vs. 'You're supporting a system of degradation'" and wrote, "Sex buyers were far more likely than non-sex buyers to commit felonies, misdemeanors, crimes related to violence against women, substance abuse–related crimes, assaults, crimes with weapons, and crimes against authority. All of the crimes known to be associated with violence against women were reported by sex buyers; none were reported by non-sex buyers."[4] Of course, critics of Melissa Farley, et al., recognize that interviewing 201 individuals doesn't make universalized standards. Clearly, the attitude of these writers is one of victim/aggressor when it comes to working in the sex trade. If that dichotomy is rejected, then that view of the men soliciting sex work must also change.

It is, however, a safe assumption that the majority of them are men. There is a niche market for women who pay for sex, but the numbers are still very small. It is men who pay for sex in a large margin, and those men can be gay or straight.

According to a study in Great Britain, there are several motivations for paying for sex, including the following:

- desiring sexual variety
- dissatisfaction with existing relationships
- sexual gratification
- loneliness, shyness, or incapacities (mental and physical)
- having no other sexual outlet
- begin separated from a partner by travel
- curiosity, risk, or excitement; to exercise control[5]

Let's look at some of these in turn.

### Masks

As my friend said in her e-mail, "My husband really liked Dungeons and Dragons, which might have been a clue." She continued, "He liked to play a role." Men who visit sex workers can oftentimes look like upstanding family men, happily married and attentive to their wives and children. However, if the wife found out, that marriage would probably shatter.

### Bonding with Other Men

Visiting strip clubs and hiring private dancers has become a norm of masculine bonding in our society. Men sometimes visit strip clubs to have a masculine outing: they drink beer, ogle breasts, and talk about sports. It's even a rite of passage—many men visit strip clubs on their eighteenth or twenty-first birthdays.

### Loneliness

Once while lamenting working at a strip club on Christmas Eve, a friend told me about a client that came in every year. He was in his late seventies, his wife had died, and his family was all gone. He came to sit with my friend, whisper in her ear, and kiss her–anything to feel connected on the holiday. "He's so sweet and lonely," she said. "I like being there for him."

## Power

For many men, sexual prowess is connected to power. Who doesn't understand this? Nearly all of us feel a charge of power if someone finds us attractive or if someone comes on to us. To be able to have sex when you want is a boost to power–even if money is actually buying that power.

## Manipulation

I like to call this group the "your rules don't apply to me" group. For every value or moral indicator, this person has a reason it doesn't apply to him. Do you think people should be monogamous? This person says, "I can't be monogamous, I wasn't built that way." They may lie, use reverse psychology, assign blame, and even use pity to justify visiting sex workers. Manipulators capitalize on your best qualities, turning them into weapons against you.

## Right to Sex

I asked a man once, "Why did you visit sex workers when you were married?" He answered, "My wife didn't want to have sex because she was too busy with our daughters. She lost interest. But I deserved to have sex, so I visited the street workers in our town." I am quite sure that his wife would disagree with his assessment, especially with the level of dishonesty that regularly visiting sex workers required in their life.

## Difficulty with Intimacy

You know, all of us come at these adult relationships a little off. Think of all the biblical characters and how they are heroes and yet do things that seem to lack integrity. King David, for example. He's God's favorite. He's a wonderful king and a mighty warrior. He is brave, generous, and loving. Yet he has his girlfriend's husband killed when she is found pregnant. When we list David's traits, we don't list "murderous," do we?

We all come into adulthood with scars. We create even more scars in adulthood. This makes us unable to love perfectly. Intimacy is difficult for all of us. Many men who visit sex workers are avoiding intimacy in favor of sex.

So the question I'd like to ask is this: can a man who visits sex workers have integrity?

My answer to that question is, *Absolutely!* Do they all have integrity? No, they do not.

When I first founded Star Light, I learned that our volunteers were angry with the men who visited strip clubs. We were ensnared in the concept of victim and perpetrator. In order to dispel this anger, I did an experiment in one of our meetings. We all wrote down the names of the good men in our lives and their relation to us. Then we wrote the names of the bad men. Pulling out both lists, we asked, "Which of these men would go to strip clubs?"

We found that both good men and bad men visited strip clubs. Many of us could see our mentors, friends, and fathers at strip clubs, treating the dancers with respect and tipping them well. We could also see some of the bad men in our lives at the clubs—perhaps not acting so well but still participating in the sex economy.

The biggest revelation for me was realizing that the man I respect the least, who has treated women horribly, would never go to a strip club. He would say, "I could never go to a strip club, it's demeaning to women!" Yet he would demean women daily, the ones he was married to, the ones on television, and the one who mothered him.

This is worth considering: Why is it that some men who have the strongest moral opposition to sex work can be the very same ones who treat women as beneath them?

No person is whole and complete in and of themselves. The men who visit sex workers are no different from you and me. We all have hurt, angry, and wounded feelings. We all seek to fill the empty spaces in our lives with different things. Some people fill them with lovers, friends, or family. Some people fill them with obsessions, sports, shopping, food, drugs, or alcohol. Some fill them by visiting sex workers. Others fill them with becoming sex workers.

What exactly happens when a person decides to sell sex? There's no universal way it happens, but there is a sort of cycle. That cycle changes significantly with the amount of privilege someone has prior to entering sex work, but the basics are the same.

The first step in the cycle is entering sex work. The decision is usually a financial one, whether it's the need of money for basic survival or a desire for more money than a person can make in a traditional job.

The second step is drawing boundaries. A sex worker says, "I will do this, but I will not do that." For a stripper, it may be, "I will take off my top only, but I won't dance totally nude." For an escort, it may be, "I will give oral sex but will not have penetrative sex." She may say, "I will always have safe sex." Everyone enters the industry with boundaries.

The third step, though, is a loosening of those boundaries. The sex worker will end up doing things she did not set out to do. Every sex worker ends up doing acts that she didn't want to do—being more vulnerable to disease and violence then she planned.

The fourth step is the decision to get out of sex work. An individual can choose to exit the industry in many different ways. She can leave all at once, start another job or project and move slowly, or keep trading sex for a long time, transitioning to only one or two regular clients. Some sex workers have found a "sugar daddy" situation that has allowed them to leave the larger sex market.

Everyone decides to leave the industry at some point. They may leave because they're tired. They may leave because they have other opportunities or want different opportunities. They may leave because they've been victims of violence. They may leave because they've been arrested. They may leave because they feel too old for the work. They may leave because they have physical limitations. When they decide to exit the industry, they can leave by themselves or with the help of others. Their exit can be abrupt, or they can slowly reduce the number of engagements they have until they have exited.

Consider a woman, with two children, who receives no money from the children's father. She has a limited education, finishing high school, but reads on an eighth-grade level. She was out of work one day too often with a sick child and lost her job. She lives in an area where unemployment is high, and in this economy, it's difficult to find work.

She has a friend who is willing to help her get started in the sex industry, who says, "Come on, girl, you can do better than this." Her friend shows her the place where she'll need to stand and what to look for when a car slows down. Her friend will help her know how to make a client happy. And, hopefully, her friend will teach her how to be safer: how to negotiate for condom use and to get the money up front.

Her first night on the street, she'll be approached by a car. She'll feel a deep rumble in her gut that says, "Not this one!" She is unsure whether the gut feeling is about this particular customer or any customer. But she'll talk herself out of her instinct and get in the car with him. She'll tell him her price and he'll agree. He'll take her somewhere.

Sometimes the first trick goes just fine. She makes some money, and she eases the anxiety she has about working. She is able to pay some toward her rent. She finds that the client isn't awful and that she didn't have a terrible time. After her shower, she feels even better.

But there's another possibility, too. I have heard many stories about the first night. Sometimes women get victimized that first night or get robbed. She forgets to get the money up front or allows the client a little too much leeway on choices, and he robs her of her time and sexual attention. Other times, she learns this in a more violent way: she's raped, robbed, and beaten. She doesn't go to the police because she fears the police or thinks that she was asking for it, that you can't rape a sex worker.

The next time she works on the streets, she does things differently. She listens when her instinct says, "Run!" She hones her instinct as time goes on. She can identify cops, rapists, thieves, and just plain jerks. She puts a community into place to help her. She finds a man to provide physical protection and promote her business, a pimp. She gets a regular corner. She gets some regular clients.

But all instinct has imperfections. She gets arrested once or twice. She begins to smoke a little marijuana or drink some to help her stay awake overnight on the streets. She likes to hang with the men, and they like for her to smoke, drink, or shoot up with them.

She falls away from the day life. Waking at four in the afternoon or getting her hair and nails done so that she looks good for her clients takes her out of the natural life of her family. The kids only see her for a little bit each day. She is tired after working at night, so they don't see her for breakfast, only a little in the afternoon and evening. New people begin entering their lives, and they aren't always people who have their best interests at heart.

Let's look at another young woman. She finds that selling sex is a way she can pay for college or graduate school—better than loans and better than depending on her parents. She works a couple of days a week. She has an incall studio, an ad on the Internet, and a friend who is showing her the ropes. She doesn't have sex with men, but she just gives erotic massages. Maybe she operates a web cam or has a phone line. She figures out a way to circumvent anyone asking how she got the money. She tells her family and friends that she works in a restaurant.

A few of her tricks go wrong, though. One time a client insists, forcefully, that she have penetrative sex with him. Another time, she forgets to ask for the money up front and he refuses to pay her. Another time, a client turns out to be a cop—which he doesn't reveal until after she's had sex with him.

Performing sex work guarantees loss. There's a level of vulnerability that comes with selling sex. There's physical, legal, emotional, sexual, and financial vulnerability that comes with the job. For some, the pay doesn't outweigh the risk. For others, they believe they'll never be susceptible to those losses, and they come as a surprise. And even others ignore the risks and the losses.

What kind of loss happens? First, there is the loss you know you'll have. You know that your mother isn't going to approve of the work you're doing, so you lose the honesty factor in your relationship. You know instinctually that you're going to lose dating relationships.

Then there's the loss that you don't know you're going to have. Most people in sex work lose their days. Life becomes a night adventure. Most people in sex work lose friends. In some instances, it's just because sex workers' lives happen at night, and they never see their friends who live during the day. Other times, it's because their friends judge them.

There are also the surprise losses. One example is the loss of friends to violence. Violence on the streets is not unusual. Another example is a lost sense of security. Sex workers do not have the protection of the police. Another example is the loss of the way a sex worker feels about her body—many sex workers feel like their body doesn't belong to them anymore or they feel disconnected from their bodies.

Sex workers can also lose their future. Melissa Petro, the young art teacher in New York City, had to resign after coming out about having performed sex work. Her attorney, Gloria Allred, wrote, "This is a modern day witch hunt. They ignored the fact that she was a successful and well loved teacher, and focused instead on her speech in writing outside of her job."[6]

Any former sex worker who has told their intimate partner about their time in the sex industry will admit that it continues to impact their intimate relationships. It is difficult to find an intimate partner who understands and accepts that their partner once sold sex. Whether it's intimidation about the number of partners, judgment about the choices the partner made, or even, for some, fetishizing the work, it brings a lot of stress to a relationship.

The worst kind of loss is violent in nature. Beatings, rape, and death are all very real possibilities in sex work. December 17 is *International Day to End Violence against Sex Workers*, and in 2009, I marched with sex workers in Washington, D.C., demanding an end to violence against sex workers. As we stood at our gathering place, there were stories of brutality. One of the most striking was a young woman who told of an abusive John: "He started beating me, right in the open. People stood around watching. He broke my leg." The police were called, and she asked that they take the John to jail. The police answered, "If we arrest him, we also have to take you in, because you were selling sex." She opted not to go to jail.

Of course, most decisions in our lives leave us vulnerable to loss. Are the losses connected to sex work worse than others? What about the workaholic lawyer who misses her children's childhood? Or the woman who marries again after her first marriage and loses custody of her children? Loss is inherent in choices. You choose one thing, you lose others. Maybe some of the costs are worse in sex work, but those same losses can come for all women—loss of intimate relationships, rape, or abuse.

For many, there are positives to the sex industry. For one, there's a heightened sense of awareness and acceptance of their bodies. Time after time, women have said to me in many ways, "Sex work taught me that bodies come in all shapes and sizes and that each one (including mine!) has beauty in its way." They also report an increase in the amount of power they feel about their own abilities. Much like a salesperson's first sale, sex workers feel a sense of accomplishment and prowess after servicing a customer. And let's not forget the power that money has! Sex workers can make very good money.

For many who have been abused, sex work is a way of taking back power. One dancer I worked with had been molested as a very young child, then again by a neighbor when she was a little older. The neighbor made her take all her clothes off. He didn't touch her; he just threatened her with physical pain if she didn't comply and threatened her family if she told. And dancing, for her, had a lot of power. Dancing was her way to say, "I decide when my clothes come off. Not you!"

For many sex workers, the sex industry is a way for them to reclaim their sexuality, to own it on their own terms and not on anyone else's.

There's also a sense of camaraderie that can come with sex work. In strip clubs, women have good friends. In activist circles individuals meet and form long-lasting friendships that can extend out of sex work and into other areas of their lives. Friends who understand your lifestyle, your choices, and your routine are invaluable.

Finally, there are a lot of skills in sex work that are transferable to other fields. Sex workers make great salespeople. They usually build instincts for reading people and for understanding economic standings and also build great skills for customer service. Customer service skills, of course, come out of the type of sex work a person does.

Talking about sex work would be so much easier if we could vilify all the purchasers of sex and denigrate all the sellers of sex—if all the individuals on the evil side wore black hats and all the powerless victims wore white hats. But it's not that simple. There are nuances to both the purchase and the sale of sex. There are nuances in every aspect of the trade. There are especially nuances between the individuals in the trade. It would be much less challenging to just choose a side and argue with anyone who disagrees. But if we do this, if we refuse to deal with the complexities of the industry and of the people involved in the industry, we will do no justice for the individuals there. To really understand and really serve, we have to understand.

# 7

## Paradise City

### *The Types of Sex Work*

And the girls are pretty

—GUNS N' ROSES

There are many ways to classify the different types of sex work. They can be classified on the amount of agency and autonomy people retain in the work, how legal or illegal the work is, how much of their client interactions are in person, which sex acts are performed, and where they find clients.

For our purposes, I'm going to classify them by legality. First is prostitution, which is illegal in most of the United States. In fact, it's only legal in twelve counties in Nevada.

Prostitution takes many forms. Some women, including trans women, solicit sex on the street, where they stroll through an area known for prostitution looking for business. Others solicit sex through back pages of publications, on sites known for trading sex, such as the Eros Guide, and on their own personal Web sites. They might include a picture, a description of their appearance, and contact information, but they rarely indicate that there is a fee because selling sex is illegal. Still others work through agencies, which can be listed in phone books and online. Others work in indoor establishments—massage parlors or brothels. Many individuals who engage in prostitution call themselves escorts, and they advertise as selling time rather than selling sex, because selling time seems to be legal.

Some sex workers trade on the street, others indoors, whether in their own spaces (called incalls), in hotels, or client homes (called outcalls). Sex workers have their own limits about the types of sex they offer: anal, vaginal, or nonpenetrative. Some do fetish work, including being submissive or dominant. Services can start as cheap as $10 while some are more expensive, ranging in the thousands. Some sex workers have managers. Some work independently. Some sex workers require safer sex, including condom use for all sex acts, and other sex workers provide riskier behavior.

The greatest risks that people in prostitution face are violence, disease, and arrest. Each decision they make can heighten or lessen risk. Being indoors significantly lessens the risk of arrest. Performing nonpenetrative sex acts and practicing safer sex reduces the risk of STIs including HIV. Having a screening process for clients—which may include getting real phone numbers, addresses, and even work information—lowers the risk of violence.

The porn industry is a different industry than prostitution because the work is legal. There are forms that have to be filled out, permissions granted, and all manner of legal protections to make sure that there are no underage performers in porn. There are legal matters that any porn producer must attend to in order to make the film, and these are subject to the law.

The legality of porn makes the industry more public. There are red carpet events, like the annual Adult Video News Awards, which is considered the Academy Awards of porn. There are industry-wide events, conventions, and fan appreciation days. Porn actors and actresses have agents and are often booked in upscale strip clubs to meet their fans. Porn stars are interviewed on television and do guest spots on radio programs like the *Howard Stern Show*. They are famous.

Because it's not illegal and porn stars are more open, porn actors and actresses are more insulated from the isolation and stigma that accompany much of the sex industry. There are some mainstream actors and actresses who have started out in porn film. Plus, there are big movie stars who have sex in movies. Why is it different? Most of the time, movie actors and actresses are acting like they are having sex. Porn stars are not acting. Well, they're not acting the sex part—they may be acting the rest!

The porn industry has been very resistant to using condoms, so in heterosexual porn, it is an industry practice that the actors be tested monthly for HIV and other STIs. Lesbian sex has such a low risk of HIV that lesbian porn actresses don't usually get tested. In

California, where most porn films are produced, there have been clinics that work specifically with porn actors and actresses.

There have been recent HIV/AIDS cases in the population of porn stars, however. In early 2011 news broke that one individual had tested positive for HIV months earlier, and he still continued to have sex on film with no condom after being diagnosed. The worst part about this is that the HIV infection is most contagious during the early stage of the disease. The actor's viral load was probably high, so sex with him was very risky.

Like the porn industry, strip clubs are legal. They are governed by local laws and regulations, which dictate the acts that women can perform in the clubs. In some jurisdictions there is a relationship between nudity and alcohol. Some jurisdictions don't allow alcohol and full nudity. Some don't allow nipples to be seen, so many times dancers use flesh-colored latex paint to cover them. Some laws require a three-inch "t-back," a thong panty. There are clubs called "bikini clubs" where the women have to wear a bikini top and a small thong. There are other clubs where it's legal to dance nude. In many areas, strip clubs cannot be close to churches or schools.

When you go to work, there are laws that govern the work you do. There is legal protection against sexual harassment. There are minimum wages that your bosses must pay you. There are rules of conduct for you, the employee, but there are also rules of conduct for the clientele. There are protections in place, especially regarding compensation if you are hurt at your workplace and unable to work. If you are a full-time employee, there are the benefits of full-time work: sick leave, unemployment insurance, tax withholding, vacation pay, maternity leave, and maybe even health insurance.

Not so for exotic dancers, or, in fact, any of the other jobs in sex. Exotic dancing is similar in nature to working in a restaurant, because restaurants have very few benefits. If you work in a strip club, chances are you have no benefits, even though the work is legal. At most strip clubs, dancers are considered independent contractors. As such, there is no minimum wage, no unemployment insurance, and no worker's compensation. As the saying goes, "No workee, no payee."

Most strip clubs go further than this. Not only are dancers considered independent contractors, but they are also charged money to work each shift. Clubs structure their payments differently, but dancers are charged anywhere from $20 to $100 per shift, just to work the shift. On top of that, there are usually fees that have to be paid based on the amount the dancer makes. If she makes $25 for a private dance, often the club will keep $5 of that money. On top of that, the dancer can be expected to "tip out" at the end of the night—giving a percentage of her tips to the bouncers, bartenders, and dressing room attendants. There are also fees for missing a shift and arbitrary fees for being late and/or being a part of a disturbance in the club.

There are a lot of dancers who make really good money. But there are dancers who end up owing a lot of money to their clubs.

There are some clubs where the owners take advantage of their power over the dancers. It's not unusual for the owner to institute "club bucks," a form of currency that the customers can purchase with their credit card, avoiding the more expensive cash advances. A hundred dollars in *funny money* would be given to the customer, and his charge card would not charge a higher fee. However, the club often took a percentage of the funny money and did not disclose that to the customer. For instance, a customer would want to tip his dancer $20 and would give her twenty club bucks. When she turned those in for the night, she would receive $18 in tips.

One stripper friend had finally had it with her club taking that unofficial cut of her tips. She decided to talk the other dancers into refusing funny money that night. When a customer went to pay her with the photocopied bills, she just politely said, "You know that the club takes 10 percent of the tips I make with this?" The club was not happy with my friend. She was fired that night.

The employment question at strip clubs is whether dancers are truly independent contractors or whether they are employees. The IRS ultimately makes this decision. They say, "An individual is an independent contractor if the payer has the right to control or direct only the result of the work and not what will be done and how it will be done."[1] Because the strip club often sets a shift, requires a dress code, and sets the fees for the dancers, many legal experts believe that the relationship between a strip club and a dancer is employer/employee. If this is the case, then strip clubs should pay a wage, offer benefits, and provide labor protections.

However, many dancers don't want to be considered employees. The independent contractor relationship allows them to write off expenses, such as makeup, costumes, and even breast augmentation. If the dancer works at two or more clubs, she can write off the travel to each club. Dancers say that being independent contractors gives them more autonomy and more flexibility in work schedules.

Ultimately, the problem with not having any legal protections in strip clubs means that dancers don't have the safety nets that society generally provides.

There are other types of sex work, too. There are cam girls, who do strip and masturbation shows while chatting with customers. A lot of cam girls work from home in front of their computer, and their customers are online. The tools of their trade are video webcams and computers. The clients pay by credit card, usually in blocks of time. Therefore, they have a lot of independence. However, they are also in isolation.

Phone sex operators are very similar to cam girls. They have conversations with clients while the clients usually masturbate. Their clients typically pay by the minute. The tool of the trade is a telephone. It's legal, easier to leave the work because there is little chance of being recognized, and the risk is relatively low.

There are also specialized sex workers who do what is called "fetish work." Because sexual pleasure is so individualized and people have many different desires, these individuals cater to the preferences of their clients. The one most recognized would be a dominatrix. She has a specialized uniform with whips, corsets, and stilettos. She is used to role play. Another would be a foot model, who will wear the client's preferred footwear, and the client will usually use the footwear in a sexual manner. Some prefer erotic wrestling. There's a fetish for nearly everything you can think of and someone willing to profit off it.

You can learn more about what sex work is like from sex workers' memoirs. My favorite is *Strip City* by Lily Burana.[2] *All I Could Bare: My Life in the Strip Clubs of Gay Washington, D.C.* by Craig Seymour[3] is a great story of gay strip clubs in Washington, D.C.. *Whip Smart: A Memoir* by Melissa Febos[4] talks about her experience as a dominatrix. Ruth Fowler's *No Man's Land*[5] is a raw story of a young woman with too much privilege, but the images of violence in this memoir may be experiences other women have had. Diablo Cody, writer of the movie *Juno*, also wrote a memoir of stripping called *Candy Girl: A Year in the Life of an Unlikely Stripper.*[6] The thing I liked about this book was Cody's spirit. She belongs to a subset of sex workers who have lots of tattoos, idolize erotic model Betty Page, and dress like 1940s pinup girls. There's a fierceness about her, a disdain for the industry, and yet a fascination with it at the same time.

I also recommend some podcasts on the Internet at http://www.redumbrellaproject.org. They are true stories told by sex workers, and there are more than fifty of them available for free. Two great anthologies to check out are *Hos, Hookers, Call Girls, and Rent Boys: Professionals Writing on Life, Love, Money, and Sex,* edited by David Henry Sterry and R. J. Martin Jr.,[7] and *Sex Work: Writings by Women in the Sex Industry,*[8] edited by Priscilla Alexander and Frederique Delacoste. Both of these collections have stories from street-level sex workers.

Even though it seems like sex workers would fit into neat little categories by work or vulnerability or amount of money, they really defy categories. There are no clear boundaries between types of sex work. Some exotic dancers perform "extras." Some escorts do fetish work. Some porn stars escort. These job descriptions overlap. The lines we draw end up becoming blurred.

The sex industry in the age of camera phones and the Internet is not as private as it used to be, even when I began working with sex workers years ago. At that time a woman could still make photos and movies without the fear of being outed as a sex worker. If you worked in a club, you didn't have to worry about a client outing you unless you gave him your phone number or real name (which most people didn't). You didn't have to worry about a client outing you on the streets because they had as much to lose as you did, if not more.

That's not the way it is anymore. Illegal photographs and videos of sex workers are taken all the time in peep shows, at strip clubs, and in client sessions. Club owners now expect exotic dancers to have pictures made and to use them in the club advertisements and annual calendars. Clubs and services are reviewed regularly now on the Internet—where the pretty girls are, which escort will do what services, and whether a sex worker's own advertisements really fit.

This also means that anyone can go onto the Internet and out a sex worker without having to out himself or herself. Anyone can do a quick Google search with a real name and find an address or a work phone number. Ruining someone's life, anonymously, has never been easier.

In early April 2011, a new Web site came online in the tradition of WikiLeaks. It was called PornWikiLeaks,[9] and it published the medical records of porn sex workers from a clinic in California where a porn star had tested positive for HIV. Not only that, it also released real names of people who had worked under pseudonyms and made it possible to connect those real names with real addresses.

A dear friend of mine called me crying. "Lia," she said, "now if my daughter Googles my name, she'll be able to pull up the films

I worked on." My friend has always known that she would tell her teenage daughter "when she gets old enough," but she's not ready yet.

The Internet makes it easy for police to find sex workers. They scan the ads or the adult Web sites specifically advertising escorts, set up dates, and arrest the sex workers.

However, the Internet does make finding safer clients a bit easier. Prior to 2010 a sex worker could place an ad on Craigslist and have a client in a few minutes. Since then, Craig Newmark has closed the adult services section, but there are still plenty of escort sites, both by individuals and by agencies. There are even sex workers and their managers who advertise on Twitter.

The Internet also makes it a little easier for sex workers to screen their clients. Many sex workers require identification, a work address, and a legitimate phone number before seeing a new client. The sex worker may even make a call to the client's office just to verify his employment.

It's always a catch-22, though. When something makes trading sex easier and safer, the chances are that it makes it easier for exploitation, too. One young woman told me about finding an escort agency online. The manager e-mailed her details for her first job. She was to meet a client at a hotel, have dinner, and engage in sexual activity. The usual rate was $800, but, since this was her first time, the manager said she'd only make $200.

The young woman met the client, performed her part of the deal, and collected her pay. Then the manager contacted her and asked, "How would you feel if your client had filmed your entire time together in the private room? Would it be OK if I showed the film to some of my friends?" The young woman panicked. She didn't want her family to know she had done this. She didn't want her college mates to know, either.

She was blackmailed by the manager. She was in a quandary. Could she go to the police? Well, technically, she could, but she would face the risk that they would arrest her on prostitution charges. Perhaps she could have made more of a case if she had an address or a phone number for the manager. As it was, all she had was an e-mail address. The video could not be legally distributed, but who was to keep it from making its way into the e-mail inboxes of a few thousand people?

Up until now we've looked at individuals who are trading sex by choice or circumstance. What about those who trade sex by force or coercion? Working conditions for these individuals can be much more difficult. They can experience more violence and more vulnerability than any of the others. Trading sex because of coercion or force is often called trafficking.

What is trafficking? The definition of trafficking is dealing or trading something illegal. Human trafficking, therefore, is dealing or trading people. The Trafficking in Persons Report, an annual report released by the U.S. State Department, says that the types of trafficking include debt bondage/bonded labor, sex trafficking, forced labor, involuntary domestic servitude, forced child labor, child soldiers, and child sex trafficking.[10] Trafficking in persons happens on a global scale, but it's very difficult to tell how many people are actually trafficked because it's an underground economy.

Sex trafficking is not the biggest portion of the exploitation that happens, although it gets the most attention. "The ILO [International Labour Organisation] estimates that for every trafficking victim subjected to forced prostitution, nine people are forced to work."[11]

It is very important to understand the distinction between international sex trafficking and domestic trafficking. When you hear about domestic trafficking in the United States, it is very infrequent for rescue agencies to be talking about foreign nationals being brought into the United States to perform sex.

Antitrafficking organizations have successfully redefined the word *trafficking* since 2004 to mean anyone who is trading sex. Rescue organizations include individuals who are trading sex by circumstance and by choice not just coercion in the term "trafficked persons." In their definition they include people who would not define their own situations as trafficking.

Coercion, like so many other facets of sex work, is a continuum. There are some who have chosen to work in the sex industry. There are some who have picked sex work as their best option because of financial need. There are some who are mildly coerced, convinced by a lie that a boyfriend or a relation tells them. There are some who are forced in but remain because of choice. There are some who are in sex work by complete and total force.

One underlying theory of the antitrafficking organizations is that all pimps are bad, and that pimps cannot offer anything to the women who work for them except violence and distrust. However, this is not always the case. Sometimes pimps offer protection, housing, advertisement, and pay a decent wage. Some pimps offer a relationship, though flawed, but perhaps a loving relationship.

There are many children who make a choice to be in sex work. However, many states set age limits indicating when children can consent to sex. Often times, children are leaving abusive homes and it seems to them that selling sex is better than being at home. While it may not be a great choice, sex work is a choice. It is often the only choice that appears viable. I believe it is our responsibility to make sure that there are other choices. Domestic antitrafficking organizations target teens who are trading sex, assuming that they cannot, by the nature of being young, choose.

Pick up a pamphlet from any of these rescue organizations and it is likely to have three specific points: (1) the number of people enslaved in the world (usually quoted as 27 million), (2) some numbers about the individuals they serve, and (3) the localities in the United States that have passed antitrafficking laws.

States are creating laws to prosecute trafficking. In early 2011 forty-four states had these laws. Most of these laws have provisions that indicate trafficking in persons includes coercion, threatening well-being and family members, drug use, force, violence, and so on. They are mostly used to prosecute pimps at this point.

Prior to these bills being passed, there were already two laws that protected people who were victims of trafficking in sex work. They were laws against pimping and laws against kidnapping. People don't have the right (and haven't had the right) to hold someone against his or her will, nor has it ever been legal to coerce someone into sex. However, there is one good thing about the laws and that is that victims of trafficking are seen as victims of violence rather than perpetrators. In the past, women who were trafficked from other countries and arrested for prostitution were prosecuted and deported, often back to terrible situations in their home countries.

Of course, the laws are not without their fair share of irony. New York governor Eliot Spitzer signed antitrafficking legislation and yet was visiting sex workers regularly. Spitzer highlights the difference in trafficking and (in legal terms) prostitution. Trafficking includes coercion and force but historically has included moving someone for the purpose of sex across a state or country line. The sex worker who Spitzer paid was moved from New York to Washington, D.C., but no one indicated that this was trafficking.

How many people are actually trafficked? The rescue movement both in the United States and internationally has an interest in amplifying the numbers of individuals who have been trafficked for the purpose of sex. From 2004 to 2011, antitrafficking organizations reported that there were 27 million individuals who are trafficked. These organizations rarely examine farm and domestic workers and focus the majority of their service and advocacy on individuals who were trafficked for sex. In early 2011, though, that number was traced back to one man who reported this number with very little substantiation in 2004.[12]

The U.S. State Department's 2010 Trafficking in Persons report estimates that 12.3 million people worldwide are in slavery. They estimate that 56 percent of those individuals are women and girls. The Trafficking in Persons Report says a smaller number of those individuals have been trafficked for sex, as few as one in nine.

You might ask why the numbers are inflated. As mentioned earlier, the antitrafficking movement has a vested interest in inflated numbers, and because trafficking in sex is, to most of us, a horrible thing, we are willing to give money to organizations to keep people from being forced to have sex. And so we do give. Generously. But what started out as a genuine concern about forced sex is now a huge money maker for nongovernmental organizations around the globe. In addition it's really difficult to prove numbers in trafficking—a number can be inflated and it can't be proven or disproved. We're talking about an underground economy. Finding the truth is difficult, at best.

"Feeling Good about Feeling Bad: A Global Review of Evaluation in Anti-Trafficking Initiatives," a report produced by the Global Alliance Against Trafficking in Women, made the following conclusion about the state of the rescue movement:

> Amidst the countless programmes and policies intended to fight trafficking and provide assistance to trafficked persons, few thoroughly assess the effectiveness and impact of their work. While resources for anti-trafficking initiatives are abundant, resources for evaluating initiatives are much less generous and are often the first casualty of budget limitations. The lack of impetus to comprehensively evaluate anti-trafficking responses suggests an innate assumption of a programme's ability to "do good." However, as this research clearly indicates, extensive evaluations have never been conducted, meaning that there is no such evidence to support this sentiment. For trafficking initiatives to be successful, they must be evidence based.[13]

Very early in my years at Star Light, I had some interaction with the American Family Association. They were building a scheme to try to keep women from working in the sex industry. They would

place advertisements in magazines about entering the sex industry–
"Work here! Make lots of money!"–that had a toll-free number to
call. When a woman called that number, she heard former sex workers telling awful stories of the sex industry.

I would be all in for a hotline that would give the explicit risks
that someone is taking to enter the sex industry, but I do not believe
in deceiving people to get that point across. The individuals I worked
with from the American Family Association believed they should
help women avoid the industry by any means necessary. But the
way a message is delivered should be in line with the beliefs of the
messenger, and Christianity teaches honesty. Shouldn't our methods
be honest?

The profamily and antitrafficking movements work to end the sex
trade, but I don't agree with their methods. Of course, the difficulty in
being critical of these movements is that I may sound protrafficking
and antifamily. I am neither. I think that trafficking in persons is bad
and that families (in whatever form they take) are good.

My critique of both movements has to do with methodology
and ideology. My number one criterion in ministering with the sex
industry and the individuals in it is this: could I say this in front of the
people I serve? The second criterion is this: Is my methodology one
that is compatible with my walk as a Christian? Am I honest? Am I
loving? Am I respectful? My third criterion is this: Am I doing good?
I don't want to do harm at all. The final criterion is this: Is the work
I'm doing changing underlying reasons that people enter sex work?

I have a friend who works for a large antitrafficking organization. They raid brothels that employ children and take the children
into custody, placing them in aftercare group homes. My friend
confided in me that the organization was beginning to understand
the negative impact they were having on the women working at the
brothels by choice. When they closed a brothel, they were affecting
the economic well-being of the women who were working there.
The children from the brothels might thrive in their homes, but
there were far fewer children in the brothels than women. This
organization was just beginning to understand that the negative
impact on the women had a huge negative impact on the next
generation of sex workers, perhaps even causing more children
to enter the industry because their mothers weren't able to work.

I think the antitrafficking and profamily movements miss the
real issues that keep the sex industry expanding and keep interested

parties from impacting change. If they keep us distracted by horror stories of women trapped by traffickers, then we won't pay attention to the fact that women still make less money than men. If they keep us distracted by statistics about Internet porn, then we won't wonder why women are still the primary caregivers of children. If they keep us distracted by stories of women being pimped, we won't notice that our corporations, focused on the bottom line, are hiring easily replaceable automatons to keep from having to specially train employees. We won't notice that these same corporations are laying off women who are pregnant. We won't notice that men are being hired in bigger numbers than women in this "recovering" economy.[14] We won't notice that they are firing women who have young children. We won't notice that childcare prices keep women in cycles of poverty. We won't notice the gender discrimination happening right in front of our faces. And we certainly won't notice the injustice, abuse, poverty, and discrimination against people of color and individuals who are members of the sexual minority.

It is these injustices that we, as Christians concerned for others, should be fighting. If there is no poverty, women cannot be duped into sexual slavery. If there is no discrimination, sexual minorities can get high-paying jobs to support their families. If there is no greed, then governmental and societal safety nets can help those in real need.

Want to "solve" the sex industry? Seek to understand its multiple layers. Begin to understand sexism, racism, ageism, transphobia, and discrimination against individuals with mental illness. Be sure to note the way those layers intersect with class, agency, and opportunities.

Want to "help" sex workers? Recognize that help has to come in the guise of opportunity for financial gain. Hire women for high-paying jobs. Hire African Americans, trans women, people who are in poverty. Honor their experience, cherish their ingenuity, prize their creativity. And put it to work.

Do not use victim language. It's important to understand that victim language not only robs individuals of their ability to make choices but also alienates them from the resources they seek. If your agency uses language like "enslaved," "exploited," or "hurting and broken," then individuals in the sex trade are less likely to seek your services because no one wants to be anyone's charity case. If they do seek your services, then they are more likely to be dependent on your agency—rather than using the agency as one of their resources, they'll use it as their only resource. And if they are dependent on your agency, they will be less likely to succeed in changing their situations and more likely to relapse.

When my friend from the large antitrafficking agency and I talked about the negative impact her organization was having on the sex workers, I suggested that she contact some of the strong sex worker unions and networks in the countries where she works and ask for their assistance in understanding how they can help rather than harm. "They won't talk to us," she said. "They hate us."

Is it not a pretty good indicator of the work you're doing if the very people you're setting out to help don't like you or appreciate your work?

Sex workers enter the industry by choice, circumstance, and coercion. But those categories bleed over into one another in such a way that you cannot say, "She entered by choice," or even, "She was coerced," and be totally true. There are as many reasons to enter sex work as there are variations in jobs. If we accept that proposition, that entering is messy, then can we accept that ministering to sex workers is messy, too? Can we accept that our response will have to be as varied and messy as the reasons people are there and as varied and messy as the types of jobs they do?

Ultimately, our response to sex workers will need to be as varied as each individual and each situation and as varied as our particular gifts, interests, and opportunities. But our response to sex workers can have some commonality. We can teach sex worker how to prevent disease and violence. We can practice advocacy and accompaniment. But our response to the individuals in sex work needs to be as individualized as the people we seek to serve.

# Section 3
# Rescue, Rebuild and/or Redeem:
# Leaving Sex Work

# Rahab's Story

## *From Madam to Mother*

When a gentleman came to see me, we negotiated a price. I priced my services high—sometimes I priced myself right out of a job—but I always knew that my time was worth it. We'd agree on a price, then we'd spend some time talking. The talking was to calm him down, get him in the present moment, get him out of his head. Once he was relaxed, I'd invite him to my bed. Most of the men who came to me just wanted to be held, or to feel the release of making love.

Except for the prince. He had other needs. We didn't negotiate a price. I told him how much he would pay me. We didn't talk to calm him down. We went straight to the bed. He didn't just want the release of sex. He needed to be dominated. When he visited, I put on a special outfit. It was black and revealing. It made me look commanding. I had a special camel whip reserved for use with the prince.

The prince wasn't free to move around in my room. He was instructed to recline on the bed. Then he was lashed to the bedposts. I used the coarsest rope. I tied his arms and his legs tightly.

I wouldn't let him touch me. I told him, "You're not good enough to touch me." He would have to beg for my attention. The prince left my bedroom with welts on his back and on his legs and bruises on his back. I always made sure that the wounds would be hidden by his clothing.

My name is Rahab. In Hebrew *Rahab* means "wide," but I don't think I'm wide. I think I'm curvy. When I was young, I had the beauty of a young woman, with long black hair, plump breasts that didn't hang too low, and a swish to my step that made men excited before I'd even said a word. Mind you, I haven't lost my beauty. With a silver streak, a curvier rump, and breasts that hang lower, I'm still beautiful. It's just the beauty of an older woman.

The people of Jericho always said, "Anyone who mentioned the name Rahab lusted after her." I like to think it's true. It is certainly true that I seduced many men. Kings, princes, warriors, and merchants, there's hardly a man in Jericho who didn't visit my bedroom.

When I got older, I moved from the boudoir to the office. I managed the women who worked at the brothel. I made sure the healer came regularly to cure their itches and to ensure they didn't get pregnant. I made sure they had food on the table. I made sure the men dealt with them fairly and justly. I trained them to keep the customers coming back for more. I did all this for a fee.

As the madam of the brothel, I helped the men decide which of my lovely ladies would best suit their needs, I poured their drinks, I made sure they were comfortable, and I collected their money. I carried their secrets.

In the years I took care of them, the princes became kings, the soldiers became commanders, and the peddlers became merchants. They told me about their families, about the intrigue in their lives, about their most secret desires.

I had a lot of power.

There's a beauty about holding secrets, because it means that people work to keep you happy. But there's a downside, too. They know you know too much. They have to keep you at bay somehow. It's not friendship. It's business. Thus I was lonely.

These people were not my people. I was someone they feared and revered. I was someone who could meet their needs, but they never asked about mine. I was someone who was powerful and could buy nearly anything I wanted. All I wanted, however, was to belong.

When the two young Hebrew soldiers visited my house, my first thought was, "These new clients picked an odd time to visit." Knowing such powerful people, I'd hear many rumors. I knew the king was afraid of the Hebrew people because he'd heard about the desolation caused in Egypt when their prophet set out to kill the male children, to set their river to blood, and to bring a plague of frogs. But that was nearly forty years ago. Maybe they had lost their power. Jericho was under lockdown by the king because he was afraid of the Hebrews, so I became concerned and acted cautiously. But they were handsome and strong looking, so I chose some girls for them.

I could tell that these young men were not from Jericho. They were dark like they had lived in the desert, not a city. They spoke with a different accent than my neighbors—like a mix between Egyptian and Hebrew. And they were nervous, like young men look when they visit a brothel for the first time. Their eyes darted. They kept their backs to the other patrons. They spoke softly. It was as if they didn't want to stand out or create a scene. I picked my young-est, gentlest women to be with them. The first time should always be a memorable time, and for scared young men, it's important they begin to feel comfortable.

Then came a scuffle at the front door. A messenger from the king arrived and asked to speak with me. My gut said that the king had sent a messenger because of the two young men, so I gathered them from their pleasures and hid them under the roof.

I received the king's messenger in my office, and he said, "Bring out the men who entered your house, because they have come to spy on the whole land."

You should know by now that I don't take kindly to people tell-ing me what to do. I told them that the young men had been here but I sent them on their way. I said, "If you hurry, you may find them at the city gate."

The king and I had a sexual relationship for many years. I know him well, and I can tell when he is concerned. Clearly, by sending a messenger to me, he is concerned about these Hebrew people. He is afraid.

The king's fear made me consider my next move, so I got seri-ous. If Hebrew invaders are going to take my country, I wanted to survive. And if I'm going to survive, I need my family and my house-hold to survive. I'm not known for my resourcefulness for nothing.

I went up to see the men hidden in the roof. I told them that I had heard of their people and of their powerful God. I explained that our nation was afraid and that I knew that the king had sent his messenger because of this fear.

"I don't want to be afraid," I told them. "I want to be safe and keep my father, mother, brothers, sisters, and the women who live in my home safe, and in return, I will make sure that you get out of this situation safely. Promise me that you will keep us safe."

The men replied, "This oath you made us swear will not be binding on us unless, when we enter the land, you have tied this scar-let cord in the window through which you let us down, and unless your father, mother, brothers, and all your family stay in your house. If any of them go outside your house into the street, their blood will be on their own heads; we will not be responsible. As for those who are in the house with you, their blood will be on our head if a hand is laid on them. But if you speak of what we are doing to anyone, we will be released from the oath you made us swear."

I helped the men to escape through the wall of the house. It's not unusual to have to help someone escape the city—I run a brothel, for goodness sake! Discretion and escape are part of my skills!

I directed them to run for the mountains and to hide there for three days. I helped them to preserve myself but also to preserve the lives of the women who served in my house. Each of them was given the choice—stay in this household or join Jericho in its death. All of them chose to stay with my household.

I had a young nephew in my family who I paid to keep watch for the Hebrew army. It was months until they came. And when they did come, they did the strangest thing. They marched around the city for six days. It was neither a fast nor a slow march, but it certainly was a march that would drive you crazy.

Every hour I checked my scarlet cord. Was it still there?

On the seventh day, something changed. The priests began blowing horns. The Hebrew soldiers marched. Seven times they circled the city. Then they all shouted. And the city walls began to crumble and our defenses were gone. The two young men who had spied on the city knocked at my door. They helped my father, mother, brothers, sisters, and all the young women who worked for me get to safety.

Now these people who follow the God Most High are my people. And now their God is my God. I no longer run a brothel, and the young women who worked for me are part of the community where I live. They call me *mensch*, a person you're proud to befriend. I am accepted, even loved, by the women in my community. When we meet at the well and at the mikvah, they laugh at my stories and cry at my sorrows.

I married Joshua, the judge and leader who lead the Hebrew people out of the desert. He is strong and proud, loving and warm, and he brings me more pleasure than I have ever known. He knows me in the way that I knew the men of Jericho—he knows all my secrets and all my sorrows—yet there is no fear and no distance. Knowing me more seems to make him love me more.

\*   \*   \*

Like Tamar, it's quite likely that Rahab was given very few opportunities when she was young. In many developing societies, sex work is a family business, so it's very possible that Rahab's mother was in sex work, and perhaps even her grandmother. There might have been sisters, aunts, and plenty more family members who made their living selling sex. To the Jews, Rahab would have been a triple threat: Canaanite, female, and a sex worker.[1]

Rahab used the small amount of power she did have (probably the support of her family and her good looks) to increase her power, to add to her agency, and to eventually get herself out of Jericho, where we can assume she wasn't happy. She was quick to believe that the Hebrew people had a better God and that she could have a better life with them.

What were the things that Rahab had to face while she was in sex work? We see she had some power and access to the king (and he to her), and she was privy to many of the secrets of the power structures in Jericho. She also had some wealth. She doesn't say to the spies of Israel that she wants to bring "her father's house," which would be typical for a woman in this society. Instead, she said, "Give me a sign of good faith that you will spare my father and mother, my brothers and sisters, and all who belong to them, and deliver our lives from death" (Joshua 2:12–13). In other words Rahab had some agency, some ability to make her own decisions and decide her own fate, and she exercised that agency definitively.

Were there downsides? Of course there were downsides! While the text doesn't tell us specifically what those were, we can probably guess. There is a strange isolation in having the kind of power that Rahab had—knowing people's secrets puts you at an advantage in negotiating for what you need, but it doesn't win you friends. What were the other downsides? She seems to feel lonely and has a large sense of responsibility for her family and household. There's no easy flight for her, no walking away from her responsibility.

When a person is in sex work, they see the bad sides of people. They see the lack of fidelity, the lack of loyalty, and the selfishness. They see people who are only concerned about their sexual fulfillment and not about their families or their responsibilities. They really see people at their worst. Perhaps Rahab saw the depravity of Jericho. Even if there had been good, solid, loving people there, she may not have seen them, working only nights and with individuals seeking sex. Whether it was skewed or right on, Rahab probably didn't have a high view of the people of Jericho.

Also, Rahab probably faced the stigma of sex work in Jericho. No one would befriend her, no one would seek her out for advice, and no one would just stop by for a visit. There's a judgment and oppression that comes with sex work—some that you know will happen before you ever enter sex work and some that surprises you.

There's also exclusion when you enter sex work. Where was Rahab unwelcome? What parts of the city were off-limits? Rahab probably couldn't participate in the religious rites, in the political realm, and maybe even in the markets. The Bible reminds us that women are judged by their supposed sexual histories. We know it from the woman at the well in John's gospel. Jesus meets her at the well at an hour when women don't generally go to the well. Jesus asks her about her husband, and she says she has no husband, but we learn that she has had five husbands. Perhaps she avoids the well when the other women gather there–because her sexual history excludes her from the normal gatherings of women.

Let us look now at those Rahab turned to for help in changing her circumstances. Two young boys sent to spy on the land. She didn't have social workers, lawyers, churches, or hotlines. She had to seize the opportunity–young men who were afraid for their lives but who had the power to save her–and negotiated for her life and for her family.

It must have been difficult for Rahab to start over. Very infrequently do we really give people a chance to start over. We still avoid them, ridicule them, and bring up their past. On one level, our remembering their history may be no more than giving directions to someone by using a long gone landmark: "The grocery store is down the road apiece, where the old shoe factory used to be." It's important to know where people come from, so that we can understand them today. But more often than not we use their history to shame them and we hold them to the same old identity. We judge people by their past.

This is unfortunate. If I hold you responsible for your past and assume that you will only act today in the way you have acted in your past, do I not deny your humanity in some way? Do I not deny you the human right to *change*?

When Christians do this, do we not deny the power of Christ? Do we not reject the competence of the Holy Spirit? One of the cornerstones of the Christian faith is *metanoia* or repentance, the turning around of our lives.

With or without a conversion experience, who among us is the same person we were a few years ago? Who among us is the same as we were in our youth? We change, we grow, and with a little luck (and some faith), we grow into better people, we make better decisions, and we become more whole.

Was Rahab offered this by the Hebrew people?

I think she was. That's why she said,

As soon as we heard it, our hearts failed, and there was no courage left in any of us because of you. The LORD your

God is indeed God in heaven above and on earth below. Now then, since I have dealt kindly with you, swear to me by the LORD that you in turn will deal kindly with my family. Give me a sign of good faith that you will spare my father and mother, my brothers and sisters, and all who belong to them, and deliver our lives from death.' The men said to her, 'Our life for yours! If you do not tell this business of ours, then we will deal kindly and faithfully with you when the the LORD gives us the land.' (Joshua 2:11–14)

Like Rahab, modern-day individuals in sex work find a reason to leave it. For some women, it's because of the awful things that can happen in sex work—disease, violence, or arrest. Whatever the reason, getting out is difficult. Is there a way we can mitigate the harms and ease the transition out of sex work?

# 8

## Roxanne

### *Advocacy*

You don't have to put on the red light

—The Police

In 2008 I attended the Desiree Alliance's annual meeting in Chicago, Illinois, a weeklong conference for sex workers and allies, with sessions on discrimination, safer work conditions, using the latest technology for marketing, and protecting privacy. Ninety-seven percent of the attendees were sex workers, the others were allies. One of the common topics of conversation was the police and getting arrested. A young, middle-class sex worker said to me, "I know I am going to be arrested. My only hope is that I don't have to have sex with the cop before he takes me in."

I asked another sex worker, "Have you ever been arrested?" She laughed and said, "No, but I came so close!" She told me the story of having been in a hotel doing incalls, when she noticed that there were a lot of police surrounding her hotel. Rather than leaving, she decided to see another client.

When the session was over, she took all her stuff and left the room. A few hours later, she got a call from that client. "I was stopped coming out of your room, and the police believe that you're a sex worker. I told them that you are not, that you're having some trouble with your boyfriend and were trying to get even with him this weekend because you found out he was cheating." The client continued, "I should have told you this earlier, but I'm a police officer,

I was off-duty, and now they're looking at me as having visited a sex worker."

They talked over their stories and agreed to never speak again. The sex worker was called in for questioning–the police told her they were trying to prosecute the police officer client–but they could never prove anything.

So what is the role of law enforcement and sex work? Many people think that the police protect the community from people doing sex work, but the reality is that law enforcement doesn't always protect the people from prostitution, nor does it end prostitution.

Sometimes law enforcement even participates.

When I think about the role of the police, I think of individuals who are paid to protect the public from violence, theft, and other things that are against the law. Police officers are supposed to keep people from breaking the law and arrest them if they break it. At least that's what I thought. In many ways, expecting the police to either protect sex workers or enforce antiprostitution laws is like asking the foxes to guard the hen house. I should be clear that I know there are really good police officers out there, but there are a few that can't be trusted.

I provided court support for a college-aged woman in the Washington, D.C., metropolitan area who had answered an ad on Craigslist for a "date" and rode the Metro out to a Northern Virginia neighborhood. The "client" picked her up in a big SUV and drove her to an abandoned construction site. He then suggested that she get in the back of the vehicle and get undressed, which she did. Then he said, "Can I put the money in your purse?" She responded affirmatively. Suddenly, the SUV was surrounded by six or seven police cars. The young woman was required to sit in the vehicle, naked, for over an hour as each cop came by to ask her a few questions. She was humiliated.

The young woman ended up pleading guilty to the charge so the drama would go away. A cop on the same force, according to her, called her cell phone repeatedly, and the police really wanted her to help them get someone "higher up" than her, like a drug dealer or pimp. She said, "I am not going to turn anyone in, and besides, I don't know any drug dealers or pimps."

Another example of police misconduct was a nineteen-year-old sex worker who was stalked by a police officer and forced to perform sexual acts for him under the threat of being arrested. This happened in Boston, and the police officer was convicted of depriving the woman of her rights. She finally got him nabbed by the FBI when she took his badge from pants as they were, literally, down around his knees.[1] He served a sentence of one year, and the sex worker also sued him civilly, winning $200,000 in damages. These kinds of victories are rare because there is so much risk for a sex worker to report a crime and to take it to court.

When I worked at HIPS (Helping Individual Prostitutes Survive), we worked closely with the police. When a sex worker needed help, the police would call us to see if we could provide services. In conversations the police helped us see that even in the best of circumstances, they walk a tightrope between the needs of their law-abiding citizens and keeping sex workers safe. In other words if a homeowner calls about people being on the stroll in their neighborhood, then the police have to respond to their demands. They have to balance those demands against the needs of the sex workers to work in safe neighborhoods.

Many of the police officers expressed that they didn't mind that sex work was happening. They just had to appease the neighbors who were complaining. In order to do that, they had to arrest the sex workers. They also arrest the customers of sex workers, but the individuals most likely to be arrested for prostitution under their laws are men in poverty. Middle-class and upper-class clients tend to use the Internet, which is much harder to track for the police. They can track the sex workers, but finding the Johns is more difficult.

When I was working with HIPS in the courtrooms of Washington, D.C., there were at least twenty solicitation court cases each week. Mind you, these weren't necessarily new court cases. Some were just status hearings for individuals who had been charged with prostitution and had been offered a deferred prosecution agreement, meaning they could execute a few conditions and have the charge wiped off their record.

Of these cases very few were males. Most were women, including trans women. There were a few men arrested for selling sex, but they were oftentimes mistaken for customers. The men who were in the courtroom were nearly always given the option to defer prosecution, which requires that they pass three consecutive weekly drug tests, perform sixteen hours of community service, and have four court dates to review their progress over a four-month period. Customers' requirements were much more lenient than the people arrested for selling. When the deferred prosecution was completed, the charges would go away.

One morning in the courtroom, there was a flurry of activity for one defendant—the defense attorney was late so the state attorney called his supervisor; there seemed to be an air of deference for the defendant. He was a military attaché from the Netherlands. He had been arrested for soliciting a prostitute. The attorneys were trying to complete a deferred prosecution agreement so the charges against the man would be dropped.

Because this white man was a military attaché, they didn't require drug tests. They extended the four-month period to six months so that he would have more time to complete the service hours, and they didn't require him to come to court for the six months. Apparently, some people have a little more leeway when purchasing sex.

Currently in Washington, D.C., it's illegal to sell sex and illegal to buy sex, but they are not prosecuted equally. If there are going to be laws about sex work—laws that make the selling and purchasing of sex illegal—then the purchasers and the purveyors should be treated equally. The law should also be applied equally to all races and all genders. Otherwise the legal system could change to more adequately address the needs of certain customers and sex workers.

Prostitution, in most districts in the United States, is illegal. I get it. That puts police officers on the legal side and sex workers on the illegal side. There are, however, different legal models, in the United States and in other countries, that work out to the benefit of both the police and sex workers.

The first model is legalization like at the Bunny Ranch in Lyon County, Nevada. In these brothels the sex workers are required to be checked by a physician for STIs and HIV/AIDS. They get checked on a weekly or biweekly basis. They are also required to stay in the brothels and not go to local hangouts during the evening and night hours. So a sex worker will, basically, live at the brothel for a period of time.

While at the brothel, a sex worker is generally required to be available to a client at any moment. When a customer comes through the door, she goes to "line up," where the client gets to choose a worker. Then they negotiate a price and do a "dick check," where the worker examines and cleans the customer, looking for signs of disease or infection. At any point the worker is able to discontinue the "date" if she feels uncomfortable.

The major feature of legalization is taxation, and the second major feature is protection, by either a manager or a government body. Sex workers in brothels in Nevada have to be licensed and examined by a doctor. The money for the examinations and the licenses go to the government. This is a tax. Also, the brothels pay taxes and fees to the local governments.

Some will say that a major factor in legalized prostitution is that sex workers are taxed on their earnings. This is both true and untrue. Sex workers are always required to pay taxes on their earnings, regardless of whether the work is legal, just like all wage earners in the United States. However, proving income is a difficult thing. Many sex workers feel if they pay the IRS for the taxes they owe, they'll be arrested. This is generally untrue. Most sex workers who pay taxes indicate that they are "entertainers" and so are not outed by the IRS because the IRS is not concerned with how you earn your money, just that you pay taxes on it.

The most important factor in legalization is the protection of the law. Many sex workers do not report when they have been victims of crime because they were doing something illegal. They worry that their history will enter into the court cases and prosecution of the perpetrators, and rightly so. Legalization means that a sex worker can call a police officer when she has been raped or robbed.

The downside to legalization is the lack of privacy a sex worker has if she has to be licensed. As we established earlier, in the age of the Internet, it's dangerous, physically and emotionally, to be a sex worker. Licenses are in the public record and make it difficult for a person to work anonymously. If and when the sex worker leaves the industry, she'll find that most employers will run a background check.

Another model for protection to consider is decriminalization. The decriminalization of sex work is just that—it's not legal and open to licensing but it's also not illegal, so sex workers would not be vulnerable to prosecution. There's no involvement of the government. This is favored by most sex worker–rights activists.

The advantages of decriminalization are similar to those of legalization. Sex workers would be protected by law enforcement and could report crimes committed against them. They could make themselves safer by choosing safe indoor housing to perform sex work, and they could have more negotiating power with customers. Some claim that street-level, survival sex would diminish, because those workers could move indoors, not needing to be picked up anonymously without doing any investigation of their clients.

Sex workers consider another advantage of decriminalization over legalization to be the lack of licensing. Licenses are a public record that you traded sex. Most former sex workers will tell you the most difficult part of getting out is that people might find out you were in sex work. It's devastating when your boss or your lover finds out you once sold sex. Decriminalization would help people keep those histories to themselves.

Advocates of tougher prostitution laws want people who trade sex to stop trading sex. I do not think there is evil motivation behind that. Many people think trading sex is a terrible thing and don't want anyone to suffer in it. However, criminalizing prostitution leads to people getting arrested for having sex, which leads to people being unable to get jobs because of criminal records. Criminalizing sex work does just the opposite of what people would like it to. Instead of freeing people from sex work, it digs them deeper in.

Some organizations, HIPS included, have offered diversion programs for individuals who have been arrested for solicitation. A diversion program is mandated by the court and is accompanied by drug testing and monitoring. Usually, these programs require taking classes on things like budgeting, job interviewing, resumé writing, and case management, which will help the sex worker to find resources that she needs, like housing, identification, job training, and the like. Usually, the courts will forgive the crime in exchange for completing the class. There's no guarantee that a sex worker will leave sex work because of a diversion program, but it does offer an opportunity to leave if the sex worker desires it.

There are other models that countries have used to deter sex work. In Sweden the sale of sex is legal, but purchasing sex is illegal. Norway and Iceland have the same model. This is the "end demand" model. Their belief is that prostitution laws are sexist and discriminate against "victims of prostitution," meaning the women engaged in selling sex. They go further, saying that the customers are the perpetrators of prostitution; therefore, they should be arrested. The end demand model holds that prostitution is not a victimless crime.

Sex workers say this is a dangerous policy because the only customers sex work will attract are people not afraid of the law. Decriminalizing the sale of sex and criminalizing the purchase makes law-abiding customers wary. Although the Swedish government looks upon the change as drawing down the numbers of women in prostitution, there is some evidence that sex work has been driven indoors and online, so their numbers are skewed.[2]

Legalization, decriminalization, and criminalization all have their benefits and their costs. The most important aspect of these systems is how the sex worker is treated by the system and how the transition out of sex work goes. In the majority of the United States, any arrest can trap an individual in sex work—filling out job applications and having to note an arrest for prostitution is an impediment to even trying to find work. And while I don't think that the system will change in the near future, it's important to recognize that there are other alternatives out there.

# 9

## So Hott

### *Survival*

I can tell you're trouble but I still want a taste

—KID ROCK

In the Spring of 2005, I was the associate minister in a congregation outside of the beltway in the Washington, D.C., metropolitan area. I had walked away from working with individuals in the sex industry in favor of working in a congregation. But Emily Cagal drew me back in.

Emily Cagal went missing on March 2, 2005. She was an exotic dancer from Rockville, Maryland, and news reports focused on the "stripper" part of her description. They put her picture on the screen and asked people, "If you have seen her, please contact the police."

Emily, a twenty-four-year-old woman, was described by one of her friends as

> the poster girl for what a friend really is. I have known Emily since 1996 and in that time, she has shown me a greater friendship than anyone I have ever known. Emily was a very generous person. If she had $20, she would give you $10.[1]

Emily was dancing for a private company, doing outcalls (traveling to the client's location) with two bodyguards. One of the bodyguards was her ex-boyfriend, Antoine Gatewood.

Mr. Gatewood has been convicted of beating Emily Cagal to death. He had an accomplice help him clean her apartment and bury Emily in a shallow grave. Mr. Gatewood is serving life in prison.

When I found out about her death, all I could think about was the impact it was having on the exotic dancers in town. News reports tended to link her death to the fact that she was a dancer, and they insinuated Emily had been targeted for death because of her profession.

This was not the reality. Emily Cagal wasn't killed because she was an exotic dancer. She was killed by her boyfriend. Emily Cagal was dead because of domestic violence.

At that time I had not been to a strip club in a couple of years, but motivated by the idea that local dancers must be scared and sad about Emily's death, I decided to visit a club in Washington, D.C. I was going to visit the club where Emily worked (the news reports always showed a strip club in their stories, even though Emily worked as a private dancer). I gathered gifts for the visit. It was close to Easter, so I chose an Easter theme—candy eggs, stuffed bunnies, and fur bunny ears. I put it all in a big Easter basket, with a condolence card about Emily.

On the day of the visit, I researched which club to go to—having only just realized that Emily didn't work in a club. I chose one club at Eighteenth and M Street in the District. A friend from church went with me.

As we drove to the club, my friend asked, "Will you mention Emily?" I replied, "I don't think so. She didn't actually work at this club, so there may be no connection." We walked up to the door, and the doorman and I began to chat.

"My name is Lia, and I'm a minister at a church in Northern Virginia. I brought some gifts, candy, and such for the dancers and was wondering if you could give this to them?"

"Why did you come here?" he asked.

I took a deep breath. "I came because I'm so sad about Emily Cagal, and I imagine that the dancers are sad, too." He relaxed his shoulders and sighed. "Emily worked here until about six months ago," he said. "She and I were friends."

"I'm so sorry for your loss," I said. We stood there for a moment, kind of lost in our thoughts.

"I'll take the basket in," he said. "Thank you."

I have often struggled with the notion that sex workers face more violence and loss than people who work in offices, wait tables in restaurants, or work in coffee shops. I don't think it's true.

Yet it seems like every time I turn on the news, I hear of another shooting in a strip club, a knifing on the streets, or sex workers who are missing or presumed dead. I have come to the assumption that the news reports these crimes more frequently, with greater fervor, so it sounds like sex workers face more violence. A sex worker victim makes for better ratings than the woman who was beaten by her husband.

Even though I don't think that sex workers are victims of more violence than women in the general population, they are sometimes targeted.

In December 2010, four bodies were found on Long Island, and they were all sex workers. The names of the victims are Megan Waterman, twenty-two; Melissa Barthelemy, twenty-four; Maureen Brainard-Barnes, twenty-five; and Amber Lynn Costello, twenty-seven.[2] They all seemed to have worked online, screening clients from the Internet before meeting them.

The deaths of these young women are apparently the work of a serial killer. Why would a serial killer target sex workers? Because as Gary Ridgway, the Green River Killer, who admitted to killing forty-eight women, said, "I also picked prostitutes as victims because they were easy to pick up without being noticed." He said in his statement, "I knew they would not be reported missing right away and might never be reported missing. I picked prostitutes because I thought I could kill as many of them as I wanted without getting caught."[3]

There's a phenomenon that happens when sex workers are the victims of violence. First, the media starts in with how unsafe sex work is. Then it follows it up with the feeling that the women were targets because they're sex workers and that the solution is to not be sex workers. The people who are killed are talked about as victims, but then they plaster their picture, their age, and their story for their viewers to judge. The deaths are sensationalized in a way that is not done with other deaths. For the families of the victims, the stigma attached to the sex industry plus the sensationalism of the coverage is painful.

Inevitably, there's some admonishment to sex workers that they are responsible for their own deaths or for any violence that happens. In one *New York Times* article about the Long Island Killer, Suffolk County District Attorney Thomas Spota said, "And their deaths are a direct result of their business as prostitutes."[4]

Well, actually, their deaths are a direct result of a killer, not their work. They had worked for a long time without this happening, and there are a lot of women who do this same work who haven't been killed.

Having the press and the general public condemn a woman after her brutal death at the hands of a sick, twisted man doesn't sit well with me.

Sex workers are targeted specifically because they have very few people who know their whereabouts and oftentimes limited numbers of people who care for them. I can't imagine any better reason to reach out to individuals who trade sex.

If they are targeted because no one notices, then, by God, let's notice!

Sex workers, tired of the disdain, derision, and disrespect given to their coworkers who have been victims of violent crime, have started a tradition called the International Day to End Violence against Sex Workers. This day is celebrated both to honor those who have been victims and to advocate for more protection for sex workers.

Started after the Green River killings, sex workers around the globe gather on December 17 and have vigils, marches, or protests. One tradition at the event is to read the names of the sex workers who have lost their lives to violence in the last year.

They are gone but not blamed and certainly not forgotten.

When I worked at HIPS (Helping Individual Prostitutes Survive), I ran a twenty-four-hour hotline for sex workers. We got calls about STIs, HIV/AIDS, violence, stalking, coercion, and other things. While we offered a compassionate ear, we also tried to provide resources for individuals in their particular localities.

One call I received was from a woman I'll call Trixie, because she lived on the border of Texas and Louisiana. She had been tricking (escorting) for about two years and was in her early forties. She was recently divorced and had begun dating a neighbor who was charismatic and fun. He suggested she charge people for sex, which was fun at first—until it wasn't.

She called the hotline because that day she had a client who coerced her into doing something that made her feel bad. He had her slick herself up with oil and act like a pig. Between sobs, she explained what happened. She said, "I know that a sex worker can't be raped, but that's what it felt like."

Trixie and I made a plan. She needed to recover from the sexual assault, so she planned a day off from her pimp. She got her nails done and recovered her sense of normalcy. Then she told her pimp that she wanted to leave. She decided to tell him while they were in his car driving down I-10, and he pulled over on the side of the interstate and kicked her out of the car. Luckily, she had the wherewithal to call her father and he came to pick her up.

We talked about the fact that Trixie would have to deal with the sexual assault sometime but that she could put it off until she was ready.

This highlights the underlying belief that many people have about sexual violence and prostitution. I don't know why people believe that sex workers can't be raped, but I think it comes from two very different propositions. The first is the belief that you cannot steal what is being given away. Because sex workers are seen as promiscuous people, the assumption is that they want sex and should be willing and able to have it at any time. The second proposition is very different from the first. That assumption is that all the sex that sex workers participate in is violent sex. Therefore, forced sex can't be rape. The assumption is that every transaction with a sex worker is rape, so the perpetrator (any client) cannot be charged criminally for the rape.

Both of these assumptions about sexual violence—that you can't rape a sex worker because either she was asking for it or she should just accept that it is the nature of her work—are rooted in misinformation. They are rooted in the idea that rape is about sex. But rape is not about sex. Rape is an act of violence. Not everyone who pays for sex is violent against a sex worker, but violence does occur.

In 2007 a twenty-year-old escort was called for a job in Philadelphia. When she arrived at the outcall, she was forced at gunpoint to have sex with four men. She testified, "He said that I'm going to do this for free, and I'm not going nowhere, and I better cooperate or he was going to kill me."[5] When the case went before Municipal Judge Teresa Carr Deni, she ruled that the charge of rape against the assailant was improper and charged him with "theft of services." There was general outrage with the ruling and with the judge's subsequent statements, especially when she said that the victim "minimizes true rape cases and demeans women who are really raped."[6]

It's not unusual for victims of sexual assault to be accused of "asking for it." When the case goes to trial, the survivor of the assault is asked what she was wearing, how she treated the assailant, and her sexual history. Sometimes these questions are used to excuse the behavior of the assailant, as if her actions made him think that she consented.

Rape shield laws have been enacted in many states to protect the rights of victims and avoid retraumatizing the victims. These provide that the sexual history or victims of rape and sexual assault are not admissible in court. However, this is not true for individuals who have been convicted of prostitution.

When we look at rape as an act of violence rather than an act of sex, we see that a sex worker can be the victim of rape or sexual assault. We see that a sex worker is vulnerable to violence, not because she was "asking for it" but rather because the perpetrator was looking for a victim. We remember that no one ever deserves violence.

And if you think that sexual assault and physical abuse are the only types of violence, let's talk about something that abuses the spirit and the body just as much: disease.

For one year in Washington, D.C., I ran the client advocacy department at HIPS. Funded by the city, my department used monies specifically designated for victims of crimes and the prevention of disease to serve individuals who trade sex and use intravenous drugs.

I ran an HIV testing and counseling center. Washington, D.C. has the highest rate of HIV in the United States. On Sunday March 15, 2009, the headline from the *Washington Post* read, "At Least 3 Percent of D.C. Residents Have HIV or AIDS, City Study Finds; Rate Up 22% from 2006."[7] There was a 3 percent rate of infection in the district, and usually, 1 percent indicates an epidemic. Those rates are higher than some African countries, where the pandemic has wrought its worst.

Stories abounded about the way people got tested in Washington, D.C. I had a friend who got tested just to see what it's like while he was training to be a tester. After the oral swab, my friend sat in the waiting area for twenty minutes. He was escorted to a room for his results. The tester didn't ask him about condom use or his partners; he just gave him his results, which were negative, then asked for his telephone number to ask him out. While this may be an isolated situation, it is inappropriate to be hit on when you're getting tested for HIV.

HIV is not a death penalty like it used to be. It's more like diabetes. Once a person finds out that they have it, it's manageable with medication, diet, and regular medical care. But being able to receive that medical care is a matter of privilege. Many people do not have health insurance or the money to pay for medications, support, and services. In many states, HIV/AIDS funding is far behind their need.

In Washington, D.C. access to those things is readily available. But Washington, D.C. is the exception rather than the rule.

The four groups most at risk for HIV are sex workers, intravenous drug users (IDUs), men who have sex with men (MSM)—which in an unfortunate discriminatory way includes trans women—and men in prison. As you can see, these groups overlap a lot. There are men and women who are IDUs who trade sex for the daily things they need to live. Since sex work and drugs are illegal, folks are arrested and sent to prison for them. Trans women who sell sex often interact with drug users who visit sex workers.

How do we stop the transmission of HIV? It's actually pretty easy to bring HIV infection rates down in a population. Use condoms and clean needles. Agency is very important to this process.

"What?" you ask. "Give out condoms and clean needles? Wouldn't that mean we're condoning the behavior? Wouldn't it mean we agree people should have sex with sex workers and do drugs?" Absolutely not. What it does mean is we have looked at reality and we know people use drugs and trade sex.

Dealing with reality trumps dealing with fantasy.

Even if you don't believe people should be selling sex or shooting up drugs, do you believe they should be given another chance? Do you believe that one day, they could decide not to trade sex or not to do drugs and should be given every opportunity to make a life without those things? How will they do so if they are infected with HIV or AIDS?

One afternoon, I was supervising one of my coworkers in testing and counseling. The man getting tested was a regular in his late fifties and had gotten sober eighteen months earlier but was just now facing some of the issues around his life. He had a partner and a boyfriend and his partner was HIV positive.

"Do you always use condoms?" asked my coworker.

He answered, "Sometimes I'm just too lazy to get up and get one."

The test results were positive, and he handled the news better than my coworker and I. We talked about making an appointment with a doctor—he already had one scheduled. We talked about discussing it with his partner—he said it would be fine, that his partner and he had suspected he was HIV positive for years. He said, "I'm ready to start treatment. I'm ready to be in control of my life."

I asked him, "Why did you choose to get tested here?"

He answered, "Because I trust you. I love you. I know you love me."

We hugged a lot. We followed up with calls, referrals, and everything else he would need.

He taught me something about getting tested for HIV. It's not about protecting yourself or protecting your partner as much as it is about taking control of your future, facing your consequences and your possibilities all at once. It is all about agency! Knowing that you have HIV is awful, but having HIV and not knowing, or suspecting you have HIV but being unable to find out for whatever reason, is worse.

The advent of HIV/AIDS is happening at different speeds in different places. It is estimated that half a million people have died of AIDS in the United States. There are 1.3 million people who died in sub-Saharan Africa in 2009.[8] Why has it spread so much more in the global south than in the global north?

There are those that say it has spread more because of poverty, women's rights, and access to health care. This means that poor people get HIV more because of lack of access to basic human needs; that more women's rights means women are having more sex, thereby transmitting HIV; and that access to medicine would mean less HIV. However, it has been shown by health officials that what really reduces HIV/AIDS transmission is talking about sex![9] This means destigmatizing sex. In countries where transmission has been discussed; where sex is talked about openly; and where it is made clear that fewer sexual partners, using condoms, and using clean needles are important, transmission has lowered.

That's not to say that increasing education, fighting poverty, and ensuring people have health care is bad, it just means that in and of themselves, they do not reduce HIV transmission. It's important to know what actions reduce HIV transmission. Having condoms with you at all times is a great thing to do, but it won't reduce the risk of HIV transmission. Getting tested for HIV regularly doesn't really reduce your risk of HIV transmission. Picking up clean needles doesn't reduce transmission rates.

The things that reduce HIV transmission are using condoms correctly and consistently; cutting down on the number of sexual partners; reducing the amount of people you share needles with; and using a new, unused needle every time you shoot up. Oh, and let's not forget, abstinence from using drugs and abstinence from sex. Of course, that's the most effective way to avoid HIV/AIDS.

It's not uncommon to hear, when confronted with individuals who are panhandling, to hear people ask, "Should we give them money?" Inevitably, someone answers, "What if they use the money to buy drugs or alcohol?"

Deep in my core, the answer resonates, "Wouldn't *you* want to have a beer if your life was like that?" Wouldn't you want some way to escape, some way to lessen the pain of what you've lost?

At the core of this question, this concern that they will purchase unhealthy products, is a prejudice that says people in poverty, in dire straits in their life, or even people who use drugs can't and won't make good decisions about their lives. In other words, these people have no right to set their own path to their life, that they have no *agency*.

How would you feel if someone took away your right to make your decisions?

Because that's exactly what society does to people in poverty and people who use drugs. I get it. Not all people seem to be able to make good choices. But we must consider how we treat people before we deem them "unable to make good choices."

When we jump to this conclusion, we fundamentally rob individuals of their freedom. I know many people will disagree, but consider it in a different way. Donny is an intravenous drug user who uses heroin daily. What do you want for Donny? You would like for him to stop using drugs, right? Well, Donny is in a court-ordered program where they tell him every day he is powerless over his drug use. He tried panhandling, but most people thought, "I'd give you money but you'd use it on drugs." There was no belief he'd actually quit doing drugs.

Because no one believes in him, Donny keeps using. It's not the fault of the people around him, but he just doesn't have any faith in himself. It's a vicious cycle.

Some people believe individuals who use drugs don't have any other choice. That's ridiculous. No one forces someone to take drugs—it is something inside that makes drug users continue using drugs. I believe everything can be different; drug users have to want them to be different and believe they can be. It's not easy. There are no easy ways out, ever, but it can be done.

Lonny is an elderly African American gentleman from Washington, D.C., probably in his late fifties or early sixties (it's hard to tell). He's married to a funny woman named Martha, and she knows the extent to which he does drugs. He doesn't hide it from her.

Lonny is sweet. He likes to laugh. But he nods off when you're talking with him. And when he's awake, he has a tick that makes him slap his own face. Lonny receives government aid, probably housing and a check, and sometimes he gets very sad. Lonny has been sober before—he got off heroin for five years using methadone and went to the methadone clinic religiously. Then his only son died.

Some days, Lonny wants to quit heroin. Other days, he says he doesn't want to face the pain of his life.

I've tested Lonny at least eight times for HIV. He wants to know if he's got it, and he likes the incentive gift card he can get for being tested. But Lonny isn't at any risk. He makes good choices about managing his drug use. He never shares needles and rarely has sex, and even then, only with his wife. It's important to Lonny to keep his wife safe. He keeps a prescription of naloxone, a drug that will counteract heroin in case he overdoses. Lonny manages his life, too. The bills are paid, he visits his doctor regularly, and he sees his children. He's only on the street to make his purchases.

Lonny is an empowered drug user. And someday, when he's ready, he'll be an empowered ex–drug user because he believes he can make choices.

Sex workers often use drugs. Some manage the drugs very well. Others do not.

Take, for instance, Kat, who was working at a strip club in Birmingham, Alabama. She was married, fit, and a great writer. She loved the money at the club and enjoyed the sexual part of the work, too. And every night she worked, she drank champagne from the time she sat with her first client until she went home. It could be anywhere from two to four bottles a night.

The drinking was taking a toll on her health. On her days off, her stomach would be torn up from the alcohol. She began making small changes to make it seem to clients like she was drinking, spitting in a glass or into the carpet. She cut down on the amount she was drinking and didn't go home every night drunk.

What would you call human dignity? Isn't it the recognition that we all have the right to live our lives as we see fit as long as we're not infringing on anyone else's right to do the same? That's what we long for on our deathbeds, right? Is it the ability to say, "Enough! I am ready to die" or "Let's not stop trying; I still have some fight in me!" But we don't have to wait until people's deathbed to make sure that they are afforded the dignity they deserve to live.

Using drugs or alcohol should not remove your right to dignity. Having a dependency, whether on drugs, alcohol, cigarettes, food, or other people, should not be read by others as "I am not capable of making my own decisions."

If we do not recognize the dignity in all, we fail to follow Christ's admonitions to love our neighbor and our enemy.

# 10

## Closer

### *Willing Participants in Their Own Liberation*

You can have my isolation

—Nine Inch Nails

The three ways you can be a Christian ally to sex workers are to fight the isolation that sex workers face regularly (what the Hebrew people did when they liberated Rahab from the destruction of Jericho); to fight the stigma sex workers face and be more accepting, open, and affirming; and lastly, to strive for economic justice in our society and world. Be willing to offer someone new opportunities, without regard to their past decisions—hire a former sex worker. Fight for fairness in the corporate world, combat unfair hiring practices, resist unjust wage differentials, make childcare a priority, and provide educational opportunities for individuals to change careers. Until economic justice happens for everyone, with no regard for race, gender, sexual orientation, mental health status, and yes, even past decisions, don't give up!

I can tell you story after story of women who have come to me with the desire to leave the sex industry. Usually, if they sought me out, they really wanted to change. If I came to them, then they were not ready for change.

Resources for change do not abound in any place. For people trying to leave the industry, there are practically no resources, unless the sex worker is willing to lie about the way she got there and why she stayed. In other words, there's plenty of money for women who say they've been trafficked or pimped, but someone who willingly chose to get into sex work? No.

What does it take to get out of the industry? Of course, it matters how deeply someone is in the industry. Finding the answers to these questions helps identify whether someone can leave easily:

How many people know that you're in the industry?

How many supportive friends and family members do you have who are not in the industry?

What other types of work have you done? What educational opportunities have you had, and are there some that you would like to have?

Unfortunately, many individuals don't have any outside support, they suffer with the stigma of being in the industry, and they haven't had experience other than the sex industry. But if just one bit of support is in place, and the desire is strong enough, individuals can get out of the industry.

This is the story of Scarlet.

Scarlet was a party girl from the time she was about twelve or thirteen. She enjoyed it all: alcohol, drugs, and fast cars. She would do anything for a good time. She started in sex work when she was about twenty-two or twenty-three. Since it seemed like she was already having sex and having fun, tricking would just add to the fun and she'd get paid for it! Her boyfriend wasn't much help in the money department, and as much as she loved him, she still needed to make a living. He helped her get clients.

On slow nights, she would call another friend in sex work and say, "I need some clients!" Scarlet would see several clients at the friend's home and make $4,000 in a night. She says, "I would do the work and then get high!"

For Scarlet it was about the drugs.

Scarlet decided, after ten years in the industry, that she was ready to quit. She had tried before, but this time she was determined.

Scarlet used MDMA, a street drug commonly called Ecstasy or X, to wean herself off of heroin. Then she used pot to wean herself off the X. That took about six weeks. Then she used cigarettes to wean herself off of pot. She decided she needed a way to make money—she started cosmetology school, thinking that hourly work and customer service is what she knows.

Scarlet moved in with her parents. She had to follow their rules, and after having lived out of their house for years, it was hard to go back. They didn't trust her after all the years of lying. So she had to be extra vigilant to tell the truth, even when it hurt. She had to avoid drugs even more, because coming home wasted meant getting kicked out of the house, which meant that she couldn't change her life as quickly as she wanted.

Scarlet is a very sweet young woman. She's instantly likable, and not in a pitiful way or in a syrupy sweet way. She's genuine, beautiful, and strong. She also understands that she can't trust everyone, so she opens up to people while at the same time holds some important facts back until she's sure she can trust you. It takes her a while.

I met Scarlet because she trusted her tattoo artist, who knew about the organization where I was working. Scarlet needed an HIV test but was scared to death about the results. We sat for twenty minutes waiting for the test to run, and she told me about her life. We made a plan if the results were positive and a plan if the results were negative.

Scarlet, with all the shared needles and unsafe sex, did not have HIV. It was the first step in facing all the consequences of her life. She got tested for STIs. She broke up, again and again, with the boyfriend who pimped her. She settled into parenting her daughter, who was already close to puberty and had been raised by Scarlet's parents.

During this transition, Scarlet's voice changed from that of a child to that of a woman. Her voice dropped an octave.

Scarlet got a tattoo that says in beautiful calligraphy, "Lord, forgive me," but God's forgiveness is easy. She had that the moment she asked. She had the strength of God behind her. When I asked her, "What keeps you going?" she said, "I downloaded the Bible onto my iPhone. I read it every day." What she needed was the strength to move forward, the faith to keep going, and the trust that things would be different.

And she did it all herself. Because a sex worker can't be saved, she has to save herself. She can only be accompanied.

Sex workers nearly always leave the sex industry at one point or another. Most tend to "age" out of it or get tired of the work and want to move to a different stage of their lives. Some get involved in relationships with individuals who don't like the work. But eventually, most sex workers will want to make a change.

After years of conversations at Star Light, here is what I say to sex workers when they ask me for counsel:

## Think Ahead

Start with restructuring the cues that trigger a person to rely on sex work. For instance, if you always think you need to pick up a shift or two when rent is due, work toward having your rent a bit early. Have savings on hand to help meet those needs early.

## Clean Out the Closet

I find that many women transitioning find getting rid of the majority of their costumes helps during this stage. Stripping costumes and clothing for sex work are expensive and difficult to replace. If you get rid of those clothes, it's more difficult to return to trading sex.

## Find a Buddy

If you have a friend who is "in the know" about your situation, give him or her the opportunity to tell you how great you are (because you are, even and especially if it's hard!). Find a counselor or a coach. Find a mentor.

## Affirm the Small Victories

Always affirm yourself when you succeed in dealing with obstacles. For example, it's Friday night, you're feeling broke, and calling a regular customer would be really easy. He'd pay you. You'd have fun. But you really don't want to do it. "I've quit," you tell yourself. When you don't call the client, pat yourself on the back. Give yourself a reward.

## Expect Grief and Loss, Even Though the Decision to Leave Was Voluntary

It's an adjustment for anyone to leave a working environment, and sex workers are no different. The grief is sometimes a surprise, though. Think about the aspects of the work you'll miss, like the cash, the attention, or the play. Find ways to get those same needs met in another arena. Love the performance aspect of your work? Try out for a play! Miss the pole? Take a pole class, so you can get the workout and the affirmation, without the headaches of the club!

## Remember Why You Left

Focusing on long-term benefits and your long-term goals keeps your eye on the prize. Ask yourself what the best part of not being in sex work will be. Here's some benefits that some women have reported to me: being able to tell people exactly what you do for a living with no judgment, feeling like they own their own bodies again (which translates, often, to better sex!), people appreciating you for who you are instead of how you look, easier relationships with significant others, and especially a real sense of pride in their new work.

Once they leave sex work, people fear that they will be judged for having done sex work for their whole lives. Will it follow them forever? Will they always be judged and excluded because of their past?

The answer to all these questions is "*Maybe.*" An ex–sex worker may be judged because of her previous work. There are some who can keep it secret, but that has its own problems.

However, sex work can be an asset. There are appreciable skills from sex work that transfer to new jobs. An individual who has been in sex work understands people, reads people very well, has great selling skills, and often is a master negotiator. She can also attract and build rapport with many different types of people. These traits are great for today's workplace.

Several months after testing Scarlet for HIV, I sat with her at a coffee shop, and we talked about how difficult the transition had been. We talked about the difference between being paid $4,000 for one night's work and $250 for a week's work. We talked about how hard it is to budget, to pay for the things her daughter needs, and how she can't buy the things for her daughter that she used to buy. She's no longer shopping at designer boutiques; she's shopping at discount stores.

It's also difficult because Scarlet no longer has the drugs to numb the pain. While there were some bad things that happened to Scarlet when she was tricking, the pain is really from the years of nonaccomplishment. She's leaving sex work at thirty-five without, in her perception, anything to show for it. There are broken relationships, tales of manipulation, and a police record.

In order to get through the difficult times of rebuilding, a person leaving sex work has to be able to redeem the years that she spent working. Redemption is really one of the most important things in retiring. When I talk about redemption, I don't mean being saved from evil but rather regaining possession of your life and of that time.

Scarlet has those standard takeaways from sex work. We laughed about the fact that she can "read" people very well. There were also good times. Scarlet had a lot of fun when she was using drugs and performing sex work. She is still friends with many of the people she knew. She also has non-sex worker friends who never judged her, always loved her, and now that she's out of sex work, she can really understand the level of care they gave her.

Of course, there were a lot of terrible things in her time as a sex worker. Somehow, the life that she lived then has to make her life today better. Somehow, the skills, the experiences, the people, and even the work have to be used to make her life richer, fuller, and more wonderful.

It's like climbing a mountain. You have to fight and sweat to get up that winding path. Your heart beats like mad when the path gets so close to the edge and one failed footfall will send you flying. The fear and fatigue nearly cause you to retreat to the safety of the foothill. But the picturesque view from the top wouldn't be nearly as sweet without the climb. The view from the top redeems the work to get there.

Scarlet is still working to find redemption from her years. It may come later when her daughter is going through similar experiences and Scarlet knows just what to say to make her feel better. It may come when a boss begins to abuse Scarlet and she's able to know it, point it out, and even survive it, because she knows how to deal with people. It may come when she finally deals with all the anger she feels at how unfair her childhood was—and she begins to reach out to other orphaned children to help them avoid her choices.

Have you ever had a moment in your life when you knew precisely how to react, how to help, and how to overcome an obstacle because of a different moment of your life, one filled with pain, anger, or hurt? For example, you know how to respond to someone who has lost her mother because of all the loss you've experienced—and how people were awful when you were going through it. You know not to say, "I lost my mother last year, too, and the pain never goes away!" because someone said it to you. You know not to say, "Well, at least you had her for a long time," when you know you wanted to have her for many more years. You know not to say, "Liver cancer? Did she drink?" because someone insensitively blamed your mother for her own death. You know that the only thing that works is to say, "I'm so sorry," hold her hand, and be there when she needs to talk, even when everyone else says to her that it's time for her grieving to be done.

When you know that, you know, in some small way, the pain you have been through is being used for good to help someone else, to spread love in the world, and to care for someone else. That's redemption.

I once counseled a woman who was date raped in her late twenties. She didn't tell anyone about it for a long time. The first person she told got very emotional and started crying, so she felt like it was her responsibility to comfort the friend she had told. The second person said, "Are you sure it was rape?" Questioning the validity of what happened is one of the worst ways to respond to someone telling you something of that importance. The third person said, "So you're a survivor, too?" That was the perfect phrase, giving the woman recognition of her own power to survive the rape but also the sense that she is not alone. Now she is often with others the first time they reveal their stories. She always says, "So you're a survivor, too?"

Using terrible experiences, even as awful as that, to make the world a better place, to make other's feel loved and cared for—that's redemption.

One of the best ways to redeem the years in sex work is to share experiences, to tell the tale. Whether a sex worker tells her story to an individual or to an audience, whether she is interviewed or she writes it, it can bring life to others.

There used to be a magazine called *$pread* that was a place for sex workers to tell their stories. Dancers and escorts would tell me all the time that reading *$pread* was like finding solidarity, receiving validation, and getting great tips for success.

Unfortunately, *$pread* went out of business, and I've not yet found a comparable publication to take its place. But there are other ways for sex workers to share their experiences. I have mentioned the Red Umbrella Diaries (www.redumbrelladiaries.com), which is a monthly reading series for sex workers in New York City. This could be done in many other parts of the country. Audacia Ray's *SpeakUp!* (http://redumbrellaproject.org) is media training for people in the sex industry so that they can have not only practice telling their stories but also knowledge about how to find safe places to share them.

Getting out of the industry, finding a way to redeem the work, and moving forward is not easy. There may be a few resources along the way, but there's no magic button or pill to take to ease the struggle. But it is not impossible. I know hundreds of women who have left the industry, and they would say with me, "A life well lived is the best revenge."

*Section 4*
*Jesus Was a Harm Reductionist;*
*You Be One, Too*

# The Woman at the Well

## *He Had Pegged Me from the Beginning*

It was a hot day. Who am I fooling? It's always a hot day here. Especially since I avoid the early morning, when all the women gather at the well. I can't take the way they look at me. Or rather, the way they don't look at me.

When I first moved to the neighborhood, I went to the well in the morning. The women were friendly, and they asked my story. I took my time getting to know them and finally told them about my life. The first woman rolled her eyes, then looked at all the other women and said, "I would never do that." The next woman had this look of distaste cross her face. It was very quick, but I could tell that she was disgusted. The others looked at me with pity. One woman even said, "You must not have known better."

I tried to go back to the well in the mornings. Every day that I went, someone sidled up to me and tried to say something to make me feel better. "Maybe there was something wrong with your relationship with your father," one said. "Surely you just didn't understand the choices you were making," said another.

So now I go to the well at noon after I've lit my candles and prayed in my home, since I'm not really welcome at our local temple. I walk by myself. I hear the songs of my childhood in my head and sometimes I hum along.

So yeah, it was a hot day. I had made one trip to the well, carried my containers filled with water home, filled my water pots, and returned to fill my traveling pots again. He was leaning against the well. I spat a little curse and then decided that this man wasn't going to keep me from my task.

I walked up to the well thinking that it would be best to stay behind the man. I began to draw water. I was avoiding making eye contact, making noise, and disturbing the man. Women here don't talk with men they don't know. They especially don't talk with men who are not Samaritan. I could tell that he was Jewish.

He cleared his throat, and I pretended not to notice. He said to me, "Will you give me a drink of water?" The question put me on the spot. If I give him the water, I'm breaking one of our laws, the law that we can't talk with men. On the other hand, if I don't give him the water, I'm breaking the rule about being hospitable. Dammit! Why would he put me in this position?

"You are a Jew and I am a Samaritan. How can you ask me for a drink?"

He answered, "If you knew who I am, you would ask me for a drink of living water."

Oh, great. Not only is he a Jew, but he's a smart aleck, too. I try to avoid giving him water, and he answers me with a puzzle. However, I'm intrigued by the idea of living water. There is no one around, and, well, my reputation can't get any worse, so I decide to talk with him. "Living water? You don't even have a bucket or a ladle. How can you get this water?"

"Everyone who drinks the water from this well will thirst again. But the water I offer will quench your thirst forever."

No more trips to the well? I'll take it! I answered, "Please give me this water."

And seeing as there's always a catch, he said, "Bring your husband back, and I'll give you the water."

Again, this man gives me two choices that are impossible choices. I can go get the man I live with and lie that he is my husband, or I can say I have no husband. One sounds as bad as the other, so I choose honesty.

I've been married five times. Each time, my husband has divorced me. My first husband didn't like the way I cooked goat and left me after only three weeks of marriage. The second divorced me after two years because I was unable to have a baby. My third husband left me for another woman. Four and five were more of the same. In trying to find a sixth husband, just telling men that I've had five husbands makes them walk away.

"I have no husband."

The man grins as if I've won the game. "Exactly," he says. "You've had five husbands, and the man you are living with is not your husband."

I sat there for a minute in silence. How did he know that? "Surely, you're a prophet," I answered. "Tell me. You're a Jew and I'm a Samaritan. Why is it that your ancestors believed you were to worship in the temple and we worship on this mountain?"

He explained to me that the divide between the Jews and the Samaritans was not as wide as I thought and that there was going to be a time when we could all worship together. He said, "God is breath, and we worship in that breath and in truth."

"I have heard," I said to this man, "that a messiah, a chosen one comes."

He answered, "That's me." Just then, a tangle of men and women came to join this man. I was afraid that I had to hurry or the others wouldn't get to see him, too. I ran throughout the town, calling on the women who I used to know when I was more acceptable to tell them that the Messiah had told my story. He had pegged me from the beginning.

I wanted all those people to know what I knew—the acceptance I felt from him. A little part of me thought, "If he can accept me, maybe they can, too." But more than that, I wanted them to know the feeling I was feeling right then.

*    *    *

It's true that the woman at the well probably isn't a sex worker. It's also true that she expects to be judged for her sexual past. And the man she meets is a religious person who accepts her fully, who believes in her power, and who not only accepts her past but also seems to actually like that about her.

The woman at the well is a Samaritan. They are a different race than the Jews, and their religion, which is so tied with race in Judaism, is different. They come from the same people; Jacob is an ancestor of both the Jews and the Samaritans. So the woman at the well is facing racism. She is also female, in a society where men and women don't speak.

Look at the divides that Jesus crossed—gender, race, religion, and even a moral line. In Jesus' time a religious leader labeled the woman at the well as a sinner and would not speak with her.

Jesus' response to the woman at the well stands in opposition to the response from the other women in her morning trips to the well. The other women at the well are given the opportunity to be friends with our woman at the well, but instead, they avoid her, malign her, distrust her, and most of all, judge her.

Just the opposite of what Jesus does. Jesus is a harm reductionist.

Because he is a harm reductionist, Jesus recognizes that the life the woman at the well has had is real and that she is a real and complex individual. Harm reduction works to minimize harmful effects, not ignore or condemn them. Harm reduction doesn't believe that the circumstances of someone's life are monolithic or black and white. Harm reduction isn't Pollyanna. It takes into account that there is potential and actual harm that comes from all of life's experiences. Harm reductionists believe that "everything is overdetermined," meaning that there are multiple factors that bring a person to where they are today.

Harm reduction seeks to understand that our circumstances are complex and multifaceted and include a wide variety of choices. Harm reduction understands and acknowledges that some aspects of people's lives are more harmful than others and that the needs of the individuals are varied and complex. Harm reductionists respect those differences and really try to meet the individual precisely where he or she is and understand that there's no cookie-cutter fix to anyone's life.

Harm reduction requires that services and resources that are provided to individuals must be nonjudgmental and noncoercive and must be based on the needs and wants of that individual. Notice how Jesus offers living water. Does he manipulate? Coerce? No, he just offers because no change really happens without the subject's participation.

Harm reduction sees individuals as the primary agents in deciding their futures and seeks to empower them by sharing information. Recognizing agency and not treating individuals as victims is very important. Victims don't have agency. Survivors do.

It takes into account that the realities of poverty, class, racism, social isolation, past trauma, education, abuse, and other social inequalities affect both people's vulnerability to harm and their capacity for independent operation. The goal is to offer resources and strategies that will meet the specific, individualized needs of the person.

Jesus' response allowed the woman at the well to trust Jesus, to seek what he could offer, to be honest about her life, and to seek answers that might make her feel better about her life.

We're never really told if this woman had long-term benefits from Jesus' visit. But I expect she was changed. Acceptance has a way of doing that: it changes us.

# 11

## American Woman

### *Taking Care of Yourself*

I'm no good for you

—The Who

In my first year of working with sex workers, I met a young woman who quit the club she danced at immediately after I met her. She had been working in clubs for a couple of years, and she was a few months pregnant. After the baby was born, she went to work at a large restaurant chain. She mentioned one day that she was having a hard time staying away from the drugs that were readily available in the restaurant where she worked. She was also flirting with a gentleman she worked with and was having a tough time in her marriage.

After checking in nearly daily, she slipped away for a few days. My mind went to the worst. "She's on a drug binge! She's having an affair with the cute boy! I must help her! She needs me!"

In reality, she didn't need me. My belief that she needed me was about my need, not hers. I needed to be needed. Does this sound psycho? Why, yes. It does. My friend was fine; she just needed a few days to herself. I did, however, realize that I needed to set stronger boundaries.

This is one of the major dangers of ministering to people in the sex industry. Or really, people anywhere. The minister's needs get in the way of meeting the real needs of the person they're trying to "help."

There are two ways to resist giving in to your needs in ministry. The first way to manage the relationship is to understand, fully and deeply, that the person that you are working with has great survival skills. She has already been through so much and has managed to survive this far. Your interruption, your intervention, may assist them in their goals, but it's their work, not yours. Your interference might make things easier, less bumpy, but the work has to originate within them, not within you. And they *do* have the power to be successful.

The second way to resist giving in to your needs is to pay close attention to boundaries. Setting boundaries is controlling our emotional responses. Personal boundaries, in the simplest form, help us know where our self begins and ends and where another starts and finishes. In other words, they help us know our likes and dislikes, our roles and our strengths, and our expectations. They help us know how we expect to be treated and not settling for less than this.

Think about it like biology. Remember studying cells? Cells have walls. Cell walls are permeable. They let the good things, like food and water, into the cell. But they keep the bad things, like toxins, out of the cell. They also keep the good things in and let the bad things out.

Personal boundaries are like the cell walls of our emotional life. They let the healthy relationships have their way, but they keep the unhealthy relationships at bay.

There are four types of boundaries: emotional, sexual, physical, and intellectual. Emotional boundaries mean you have the right to feel like you feel. Intellectual boundaries mean that you alone have the right to think what you think, believe what you believe, and learn what you learn.

Physical boundaries designate that you have a right to physical safety and to your physical space. Individuals have different needs for physical space. If you are a hugger, the presumption that everyone wants a hug is incorrect. I have heard women say, "She needs a hug. Even if she doesn't want it, she needs to learn that she is loved." But a hug, to a nonhugger, is an invasion of space and boundaries.

Sexual boundaries say that you have the right to determine who touches you in a sexual manner. These become particularly significant in working with sex workers. Not only does every sex worker still have the right to determine who they are with sexually, but they also are particularly sensitive to it. Sex workers often don't believe that they can be raped. More than once, I've heard on the hotline, "I can't be raped! I'm a hooker!" after a client has raped a sex worker.

Sexual boundaries are also very important for the volunteer, advocate, or ally of sex workers. Because sex workers are used to relating to others in a sexual way, often they will receive friendship as a sexual advance. It is your job, as the ally, to remember your appropriate boundaries and resist any sexual advance. Remember that it's a compliment, and just say, "Thank you, but no."

But it's also important to realize what seems like a sexual advance to you may not be at all. Sex workers live in a world where everything is hypersexual, so they may not think undressing in front of you could be interpreted as sexual.

Being an ally or advocate to sex workers means we have to be very clear about who we are, especially in this relationship, and what our role is. Are we friends, girlfriends, mentors, advocates, allies, mothers, pastors, enablers, rescuers, or pleasers?

Part of understanding our boundaries means respecting others' boundaries. Just like the woman who says, "She needs a hug, whether she wants one or not," we have to respect that other people are not just like us.

Ask whose needs are being met by your actions.

Boundaries, like cell walls, are permeable and ever changing. There are healthy and unhealthy boundaries. Healthy boundaries protect us from most bad things and let in most good things. There are two types of damaged or unhealthy boundaries: too weak and too strong.

Individuals with no boundaries are easy to pick out. They trust you immediately with personal information. This is the cashier at the grocery store who tells you that her husband just left her for the babysitter and she's suing him for divorce, and she's so upset she's crying on the floor every night. If you find yourself thinking, "Awkward!" you're probably with someone with no boundaries.

The other type of unhealthy boundaries is walls. This is when the boundaries are so rigid that nothing, neither good nor bad, comes through. This is the individual you have known for years but don't know much about or the individual you have known and loved for years but doesn't ever hug. Walls are not always as they seem, though. Many people can interact as if they do not have walls but still not share anything of themselves.

We all have reasons to have damaged boundaries. Someone at some point has violated our space, our emotions, our sexuality, and/or our mind. But it is the choice that we make that defines us:

remain open to all interactions, whether good or bad; close ourselves off completely; or be open to good interactions and closed to bad.

We've been walking around in our skin for a long time, and changing those boundary patterns is difficult and causes chaos in our relationships for a time. If your mother is always ridiculing you for being overweight and you finally draw a metaphorical line in the sand and say, "No more!" chances are she will feel offended and your relationship will be affected. It may even get worse. But there's the possibility that she won't make fun of your weight anymore.

With teams I've trained, I have set very clear boundaries around the relationships they build. I cannot set a boundary around their role, their personality, or their emotional energy. But I can (and do!) set some boundaries to help the relationship be balanced. These include the following:

1. no direct exchange of money
2. no using drugs together
3. no sexual relationship of any sort

It is important to set limits and to be clear with the worker about what is OK and what is not OK. Limit setting also requires the assertiveness of a worker to be able to say "no" without feeling guilty.

When I'm training about boundaries, I use a worksheet to determine what appropriate boundaries would be for a given relationship and circumstance. The worksheet asks, "What will be the benefits if I respond with a yes?" The worksheet also asks to consider the opposite, "What are the benefits if I answer no?"

Let's look at a real-life situation.

Early on in Star Light's founding, a woman who was working as an exotic dancer called me. The club where she worked was having a difficult time—a new club had opened close by and business was way down. The dancer was having a hard time paying rent. She asked if Star Light could loan her $100 to make the rest of her rent.

Now, clearly, according to our rules about giving money to sex workers, this would be a violation. However, she was a good, trustworthy participant. I know it took a lot for her to ask me for the money.

The pros of giving her the money were the following:

- It increases her trust, and she knows Star Light will be there when she needs something.
- It increases the community's trust because the dancer will tell other dancers.

- It creates a sense of indebtedness, so perhaps Star Light will have better access to the club and other dancers.
- It avoids all issues of homelessness, as the dancer will have her rent paid.
- There will be a story to report to funders of the tangible ways Star Light is making a difference.

The following are the cons:

- It creates the expectation that Star Light gives money.
- It could result in other dancers asking for money when they might not need it.
- It breaks the rules.
- It might cause the dancer to rely on Star Light rather than her resourcefulness.
- It can create resentment in the dancer by setting up Star Light as the "haves," and her as the "have not," as charity often does. When people are given charity, the relationship becomes uneven, and the dancer will resent being the lesser.
- It doesn't solve any long-term issues, such as not having enough money for rent.

In some ways the pros outweigh the cons. Building trust, at the founding of Star Light, was the most important work we could do. But ultimately, we decided that giving the dancer the money would hurt both Star Light and the dancer in the longer run, because those cons outweighed the temporary fix of paying her rent. Looking at the pros and cons, though, helped highlight that the decision wasn't an either/or decision. There were other options.

While Star Light couldn't give the dancer the money, we brainstormed some ways that she might be able to make more money dancing. We talked about picking up more shifts, getting to work earlier (the earlier a dancer showed for a shift, the less she had to pay in club dues), and working at another club out-of-town for a few weeks. We also talked about some resources for short-term help. After identifying a church with a rental help program, the dancer was able to get the money to pay that month's rent.

By finding a middle ground, we were able to build trust and encourage the dancer to rely on her resourcefulness.

There are four emotional responses within ourselves to keep an eye out for when we're looking at boundaries. The first is the desire to make everything OK. When people called the HIPS (Helping

Individual Prostitutes Survive) hotline with really awful things going on in their lives, the automatic response of most of us was to say, "Everything is going to be OK." The reality is that not everything is going to be OK. Sometimes things don't work out. And if you tell someone they are going to be fine, you may be lying.

You can't ensure that everything is going to be OK, and nothing that you do will make it OK. All you can do is walk alongside the person in pain, not fix.

The second emotional response to keep an eye out for is the need to be needed. We all know people like this (heck, we've probably been like them at times). They do not have *reciprocal* relationships of give and take so much as *rescuing* relationships—all take. The relationship partners will have great need, more often than not, but when that changes, the "needer" leaves.

The third type of emotional response to keep an eye out for is idealism. A relationship will never be ideal. If one is unsatisfying to you, then it may always be. For instance, if you're mentoring a young woman and dreaming of the day when you won't be the mentor but the best friend, you will be disappointed. Relationships often stay in the form they start, and transitioning to an equal friend relationship is very difficult after being in an unequal relationship.

The final type of emotional response to watch out for is control. If you believe that you can control and change your relationship partners, you will be sorely disappointed. The only person you can change is yourself.

Did that register? The only person you can control is yourself. And in order to work with sex workers, you should be able to control your feelings and thoughts. A key way to do this is to communicate your needs and expectations to your ministry partners, your life partners, your friends, and your family.

Easy peasy, right?

But communication isn't easy for anyone. None of us is great at it, and it takes practice to develop the kind of skills needed. But working on this skill is one that pays off, both in our work and in our personal lives.

Here are four things to add to your communication repertoire: open-ended questions, affirmations, reflective listening, and summarizing.

## Open-Ended Questions

If you and I are in a conversation, which of these questions is likely to keep the conversation flowing? "Do you like rock 'n' roll?" or "What kind of music do you like?"

The second question leaves space for the other person in the conversation to tell you, in detail, what kind of music they like. "Well, I like the Cranberries, the Cure, Coldplay, and Eric Clapton," the person might respond. The first question invites an answer, "Yes."

But it's like second nature to ask close-ended questions. (Don't you think?)

Open-ended questions are questions that cannot be answered with a "yes" or "no." They encourage people to talk about whatever is important to them. They help establish rapport, gather information, and increase understanding. Open-ended questions invite others to "tell their story" in their own words. They do not lead people in a specific direction. Open-ended questions should be used frequently, though not exclusively, in conversation.

Certainly you know people who are good at open-ended questions. They are the people that you meet who ask questions like, "Tell me about your family." They might ask a close-ended question like, "Do you have any siblings?" but then they quickly follow up with, "What is your brother like?"

At a Center for Disease Control–sponsored training, a leader told us about her habit of engaging people in airports with open-ended questions. She found that striking up this type of conversation made her conversation partner feel good about themselves. And she also got great practice for communication. She would just keep asking open-ended questions until one of them had to leave to make their connecting flight.

"Where are you heading from this airport?"

"Why are you traveling there?"

"What will you do when you get there?"

"Who will you see when you're in that city?"

"When do you expect to get there?"

"How will you travel while you're in the city?"

Notice how these questions start with "who," "what," "when," "where," "how," and "why." Open-ended questions don't usually start with "do" or "are." "Do" and "are" questions have one word answers (usually yes or no).

## Affirmations

Affirmations are statements and gestures that recognize strengths and acknowledge behaviors that lead in the direction of positive change, no matter how big or small. Affirmations build confidence in one's ability to change. To be effective affirmations must be genuine and congruent.

You're so great to have stayed with this discussion of communication!

See? I just did it there. Affirmations matter.

## Reflective Listening

Reflective listening starts with the belief that the capacity for self-insight, problem solving, and growth resides primarily in the speaker. This means that the central questions for the listener are not "What can I do for this person?" or even "How do I see this person?" but rather "How does this person see themselves and their situation?" Reflective listening helps the speaker identify solutions and understand themselves and their situation more clearly.

The key to reflective listening is to be a mirror for the speaker, to reflect back to them what they are saying, so that they can fully understand their own thoughts.

## Summarizing

Summarizing a conversation is very important. Everybody wants, especially, to be heard. When you summarize a conversation, the speaker knows he or she has been heard.

At HIPS my department was responsible for a twenty-four-hour crisis hotline. While most of the calls were related to HIV prevention, there were genuine calls from genuine sex workers who needed someone to talk to. There was one woman who called regularly to discuss her decisions about getting into porn work in California.

At first, she called to ask some specific questions, like "Is it normal that the director wanted to have sex with me before he cast me for a part?" And while I don't know if that's normal or not, my response was always, "How was it for you? Did it feel OK to you?"

I also pointed her to resources in her area, such as health professionals or other sex worker organizations, so that she might get a better idea of what's "normal" and what's not.

But the question she really wanted answered was, "I liked it, is that OK?" Again, I cannot answer that question for anyone. "Was it OK for you?"

At the end of each conversation, I would say to her, "What I hear you saying is that you are OK with what happened [having sex with the director, doing a sex act on camera, publishing naked photos of yourself], but you are conflicted about what other people will think about it." She would take a deep breath.

"Yes. I am worried that other people will judge me for what I've done." At that point, she would get off the phone. She just needed to know that she was heard.

One of the greatest tools in your relationship toolbox is to have an understanding of how change works in our lives. In the book called *Changing for Good: A Revolutionary Six-Stage Program for Overcoming Bad Habits and Moving Your Life Positively Forward,* James Prochaska, John Norcross, and Carlo DiClemente explain the six stages in the cycle of change:

- precontemplation (not currently considering change)
- contemplation (thinking about thinking about making change, sitting on the fence, wanting to change, and not wanting to change)
- preparation (emotionally compelling reason to change, testing the waters)
- action (engaging in actions to bring about change)
- maintenance (continued commitment to sustaining new behavior)
- relapse or recycle (resumption of old behaviors, very normal)[1]

There are specific realizations and steps in each of these stages that help sustain and strengthen change.

In all the stages of change, what is always in focus is that the choice belongs to the individual who is changing and that some ambivalence is normal. Even when we are most successful at changing, we can miss the behavior we've left behind. The key to changing is to accept that it's hard and that we can do it.

The stages of change can encompass many different choices we make, from quitting smoking and cursing to adding a contemplative time to our days or working on building a relationship, any change we undertake involves these stages of change. We just don't notice the fun ones as much!

When it came to changing their work or careers, most people I met working on the streets and in clubs were in the precontemplation stage. They knew that what they were doing wouldn't last forever, but they weren't even thinking about trying to change. In the precontemplation stage, a person is aware of the downsides to their behavior, but they don't care. If someone calls them out on their behavior, they are likely to want to do the behavior more.

But when someone moves into the contemplative stage, he or she will think about the behavior a lot. He or she may be overwhelmed by the idea of changing or even think that they're not capable of changing. A smoker in precontemplation thinks about quitting nearly every time they light a cigarette. He or she will be aware of the health risks and about the specific ways his or her behavior is impacting his or her life.

During the preparation stage, the person seeking change will do just that: prepare for change. It's important to identify and prepare for obstacles, find social support, figure out your best course of action, and take small steps toward change. The groundwork is laid during the preparation stage, and very often the success of changing the behavior is due to the amount of preparation done. To continue with the quitting smoking example, the person who wants to quit can find someone else who has quit successfully, research success rates of different programs like nicotine replacement or hypnosis, find a support group, or talk to a physician about changing. It's important to identify what the benefits and the drawbacks to quitting will be and to plan accordingly. Also, rewards should be plotted during this stage.

The action plan begins as soon as the behavior change begins. Action starts with the first cigarette that is declined, the first cuss word that doesn't get said, or the first drink that isn't taken.

Success in the action stage is determined by how well the preparation stage was completed. For instance, you're quitting smoking, but you really, really want a cigarette. What have you prepared for when you are facing a craving? Do you have a friend to call? Do you have a piece of nicotine gum? What are your other strategies? Do you have a list in your pocket outlining the reasons you want to quit? Do you have carrot sticks to satisfy your oral fixation?

The action phase lasts as long as it should. When you're quitting smoking, you may need that list of resources every day for a month, every month for a year, and every year for a decade. Quitting a behavior is as individualized as the behavior is. The action phase often requires behavioral modification that is seemingly unrelated to instituted change. For instance, you may have to avoid alcohol if you're quitting smoking because alcohol may be a trigger for smoking.

Eventually, though, with continued success an individual moves from action to maintenance. The maintenance phase indicates that you are successful in quitting or adding behavior, but you're continuing to succeed. It doesn't mean that there's no struggle, but where the struggle was ongoing and difficult during the action phase, in maintenance, it's easier.

It's easiest to understand this model as a spiral—it starts with precontemplation, then cycles to contemplation, preparation, action, and maintenance. In reality, though, these actions don't always happen linearly. You can jump from precontemplation to action, preparation back to contemplation. And at any moment in the process, you can relapse.

But unlike the twelve-step models, in this change model, you don't go back to day one if you relapse. Instead, you may only go back one stage or you may cycle all the way back. It depends on the individual and on the depth and breadth of the relapse. Relapse is a part of the cycle, an important part, because it shows the gaps in our preparation stage. If you relapse and have a cigarette or a whole pack, identifying triggers and putting a plan into place to not fall for that trigger again is important.

When people who want to change behavior understand this model, it helps them see that they are not alone, that changing is not impossible, and that success is within reach. In user-friendly terms, the cycle is (1) not thinking about change, (2) thinking about change, (3) getting ready, (4) doing it, (5) keeping it up, and (6) slipping up. Doesn't having a "slip up" sound better than "relapse"? That is the emphasis that harm reduction puts on a relapse—it is not more than a "slip up" because it can be easily mended if it doesn't send a person into a spiral of failure.

In helping relationships, understanding these stages of change can be very important because identifying a participant's phase gives you steps to help them. For instance, when I was contemplating and preparing to quit smoking a few years ago, a friend asked me some important questions that helped me make it through some tough things. She asked, "What are the reasons you want to quit?" I listed off fifteen benefits to quitting, and she encouraged me to write them down. She asked, "What will you do if you really want a cigarette?" When I couldn't come up with an idea, she said, "You can call me or text me, and we can talk about it." She asked, "What method will you use? Because all nicotine replacement is not created equally." We talked through the options and figured out which one would be best for me (I chose gum because I liked getting out the cigarettes, the anticipation, and the rush of nicotine).

Without her help, I certainly would have succeeded, eventually, at quitting smoking. However, through her encouragement and preparation, I was able to quit more easily, to get discouraged less (because I didn't slip up as much), and to lessen the pain of quitting.

It's easy to see why helping relationships are beneficial in our lives. That's not just for sex workers! Individuals who are the helpers in helping relationships need help, too!

Star Light had a volunteer one time who, upon hearing about Star Light, said, "That sounds just kinky enough for me!" There are all kinds of reasons people choose to reach out to sex workers. She saw visiting clubs and getting to know people as an adventure. She had a son who was gay, and she had fought the stigma alongside him, she had perfected seeing people as multifaceted and fascinating, and she had a great way with people. She was friendly, kind, and real.

Like many of Star Light's volunteers, she was amazed at the level of stigma attached to sex work but also the level of stigma attached to reaching out to sex workers. If you reach out to sex workers, people will look at you like you are crazy. They will assume one of two things: first, that you are a Captain Save-a-Ho, intent on rescuing individuals in the sex industry, and second, that you were in sex work at one point.

Fighting those perceptions can be hurtful and confusing. My worst experience was at a pastor's retreat early in my ministry. At least eight pastors, in the course of a day, asked, "Were you a prostitute?" And of course, they looked at my chest while they asked. Another ten or so asked, "Ministry to sex workers? Can I come along?"

Clearly, as I learned later, these presumptions are really about the people making them. These male responses were about their immaturity, their discomfort with sex, and their perception of sex workers more than anything else.

I began to preempt those conversations and often times just avoid them. When confronted with a room full of middle-aged, white pastors, I often say, "I am a pastor to individuals who trade sex for something they need." Most of them look at me with a confused look—I say it again and let them be confused. Some of them get it and still say, "Can I come?" After many years of responding defensively, I finally understood that this humor was just a way for these pastors to deal with their own conflict around sex. I usually just laugh and say, "With a lot of training!"

It's not that people don't have meaningful conversations about the topic of ministry to sex workers, though. One pastor told me, very thoughtfully, about the wedding he did for an exotic dancer. She had revealed her work to him, and she still felt comfortable with him. Her bridesmaids were all her coworkers.

On the eve of the wedding, at the rehearsal the bridesmaids all danced their club routines down the aisle. One dancer crawled down on her hands and knees. Instead of being shocked or upset, the pastor was friendly, laughing, and appreciative of the dancers. He didn't engage their sexuality but instead engaged them in a fun, accepting way. When we talked about the wedding, he said to me, "Isn't this exactly how the church should be?"

Anyone who is in sex work exposes her most vulnerable side to clients regularly, which makes self-care one of the most important skills in sex work. What are good self-care practices? Some examples include taking care of daily issues, paying bills, keeping up with friends, learning new things, staying active, and enjoying life.

All of us need self-care, not just sex workers. It's also really important to understand what happens in our emotional lives, to recognize feelings, and to understand thoughts. It's important to see how those things are working out in our lives. Did you yell at your boyfriend a lot, but you're not really mad at him? This can be an unresolved feeling coming out, loss that you haven't dealt with, or even some depression poking its head through.

If our emotional lives are acknowledged, our feelings validated, and our physical well-being protected, we make truer life decisions and feel more whole. Self-care is how all of us do that. What are examples of self-care?

First and foremost self-care encompasses taking care of your emotional well-being. It means speaking up when you're angry, crying when you're sad, and laughing when you're happy. And it means taking responsibility for your emotions. It's not, "You made me feel this way," but, "When you do [whatever behavior], I feel like this." Our emotions are our responsibility.

Second, self-care includes taking care of your need for time with people or time without people. The extroversion/introversion scale measures two things. The first is, "Where do you get more energy, from being alone or being with people?" and the second is, "When you make a decision, do you make it internally or externally?" Extroverts get more energy from being around people. Introverts get more energy from being alone. Extroverts make decisions by talking them out. Introverts make decisions inside their heads.

If you are an extrovert, you must schedule time to be around people, to get out of your head, and to process your emotions and decisions. If you are an introvert, you have to schedule time to be alone, to sift through your thoughts and feelings.

Third, self-care involves taking care of your physical body. Exercise, eating right, not abusing your body too much with alcohol and drugs, getting enough sleep, and visiting the doctor and the dentist regularly are all important.

Self-care also includes doing the things you have to do every day or week, like laundry, paying bills, brushing your teeth, cleaning your house, or making your bed. It seems silly, but we feel so much better taken care of if we slide into a made bed at night. We feel so much more together if we know how much money is in our checking account.

Next, self-care includes doing things that pamper you, such as a massage, a manicure or pedicure, a walk in the park, or bird watching. Whatever it is that gives you energy, makes you feel more whole, has to be scheduled regularly.

And finally, we have to have some creativity in our lives. Do you love fabric? Sew! Do you love vehicles? Change your oil! Do you love fiber? Knit or crochet! Whatever your passion, make sure that you follow it creatively.

When it comes to ministry, providing opportunities for sex workers to do self-care is a way of showing that you value them as people.

In my first months of Star Light, we began a yoga class for dancers. My thinking was primarily to find a way to connect with the dancers and to create a safe space to work out and have fun. But it turned into a great time to be in tune with our bodies. We laughed at how short my arms are, since I couldn't even touch my toes. We giggled about how different our bodies are. We noted that yoga might prevent injuries on nine-inch heels.

We took gifts into the clubs, and these always revolved around the idea of self-care. Nail polish, journals, or relaxation pillows, all the gifts were made to remind the dancers to take care of themselves. And vicariously, to remind the volunteers how important it is to take care of ourselves.

So in your toolbox for working with people in sex work, you will have several tools. You'll know why you are there, you'll know what healthy boundaries in this type of ministry entail, you'll be an effective communicator, you will understand the stages of change, and you will practice self-care.

Those are the nuts and bolts of ministry. But there is a larger piece to this, too. When you have worked with people who are in sex work, you will begin to understand the larger issues at stake here. Our world is divided between people who have and people who have not. And as you get deeper into ministry, you begin to understand this divide more and more.

You cannot be silent anymore.

I had a dream a few years ago. I was hanging out in a brothel that was being raided by the police. The police started rounding up all the women there, me included. I kept thinking, "I'm a minister, not a sex worker." And then I would think, "I can prove it!" Then I realized I could not prove it. I had nothing on my person or in my purse that proved I was a minister. I was handcuffed and taken away. I remember being resigned to this, to not fighting my way out of it, because this is what sex workers face all the time.

When I awoke from the dream, I knew something was different.

Maybe it's only a tiny shift, but it's a shift nonetheless.

I have worked, since the inception of Star Light, toward understanding sex workers as whole people, as bright and shining women and men who are powerful agents in their own lives. But in all honesty, when I started this ministry, I thought there was a difference between me and the sex workers. I believed I could help. Mind you, it was never a sense that I knew what was right for any person, never that I knew what was best, never that I had all the answers, but it was, perhaps, that I had more experience, more networks, and more maturity, and I could help. Basically, I thought that I was better than sex workers, even if only in degrees.

In my immaturity, I committed the sin of "othering," especially when it came time to talk about the ministry I was doing. I talked about statistics, the kind the rescue movement uses, judging the customers of sex harshly. I used the "these poor women" tactic, because it was the only one I knew. I shudder now when I think about talking about some of the sermons and teaching I did. I try to imagine myself saying those things in front of the women I work with, and I just can't imagine it.

I saw sex workers as "other," and that is a sin.

I perpetuated that othering through conversations, preaching, and teaching.

I am convinced that the church is replete with well-intentioned people who are committing the sin of othering through their mission endeavors. Church members are concerned with the sin of commercial sex, but, really, it keeps them cozy in their feeling, "I'm better than you." Failing to understand this and failing to point this out put me in collusion with their sin.

Toward the end of Jesus' ministry on earth, he begins explaining to his disciples that he's going to be killed. Then he says, "I no longer call you servants because a servant does not know his master's business. Instead, I have called you friends."

Jesus clearly has a shift in his understanding of who the disciples were. It's a shift from "I'm better than you" to "I'm equal to you and you are equal to me." It says, "I no longer teach, I learn also. I no longer comfort; I am comforted also. I no longer lead, but I am also led." There's a healthy reciprocity in the relationship.

There's a complex line of doing ministry that comes into play when we think about othering sex workers. Clearly, recognizing that individuals in sex work may need someone to reach out to them, someone to accompany them, and someone to help them identify resources to fill their needs, in some way, indicates that we've othered them.

Yet there has to be a way that we can justify "ministry," even if we don't think that sex workers are "worse off" than we are. So how do we do this?

Instead of looking at sex workers as the ones with the problem, we need to look at church and society as the ones with the problem. Society and the church have decided that sex workers are outside the realm of people offered acceptance. Because sex workers are excluded, we reach out to them. Not because they "need" us but because, ultimately, we need them. We need a world where every voice is heard, every person is cared for, and every outsider is inside. Because without sex workers calling us to a better place, we will not notice that our world is out of whack, that justice is not meted out equally, and that discrimination is running rampant in our society.

We as Christians have to work for justice. Look around you. Is your church composed of white, middle- and upper-class folks? Where is your church spending your money? Is it on carpet and chandeliers or on people, meeting their real needs? And what about the pulpit? Is your minister concerned with changing the world? Bringing justice to the world? Or is he or she concerned with keeping the status quo, making sure that those with power keep the power?

Then look in your neighborhood. Ask the same questions. Where are the people in need? What are you doing to make sure that their needs are being met?

I have a friend who lives in a neighborhood that she thought was going to gentrify. She and her husband have a beautiful home and now have two children. In the alley behind her house, my friend finds used condoms and discarded needles. We've talked, over and over, about her need for safety and her children's safety and how she would like for the sex workers to go somewhere else. I've argued that pushing it to another neighborhood might make the work more unsafe for the women. Where's the common ground? And how can we love our neighbors who are sex workers strolling in our neighborhood?

I don't know the answer to this question. I see both sides. I have recommended that she put up hazardous waste disposal boxes on her fence, to make the neighborhood safer for her and for the women working there. She thinks that will just encourage the trade.

What about in your job? Where are the people in need? What are you doing to make sure that their needs are being met? What are the hiring practices where you work? Are there opportunities for people who have varied experience?

Nothing will change if we don't try.

End racism. End sexism. Demand equal opportunities for education, health care, and jobs—in addition to the basics of shelter and food.

The calling implied in the statement "I [heart] sex workers" is a calling to love everyone and to offer everyone choices, accompaniment, and an end to stigma.

So far, we've learned about sex work and the needs of sex workers. Now I'm going to give you the nitty gritty, how to do outreach to sex workers so you can get to work.

# 12

# Your Own Personal Jesus

## *Harm Reduction 101*

Someone to hear your prayers

—Depeche Mode

I have made more mistakes than I would like to remember in working with sex workers. The first was that I assumed that the individuals in sex work were victims and that the individuals who were purchasing sex were the oppressors. The second was my belief that, given the option, all the individuals would leave the industry if they had a clear, supportive way to get out. And third, I believed that I had the answers for these folks.

And then I was schooled by sex workers.

I learned that everything I thought was wrong. I learned that my language had to be loving and accepting. I learned that sex workers won't come to you but that you have to go to them. I learned that *metanoia*, the complete "turning around" of a life, happens incredibly infrequently, if at all. I learned that sex workers know more about their lives than I could ever teach. I learned that change had to be motivated from within. I learned that all I could do was support a person in the changes that they desired, not the changes I desired. I learned that there are no easy transitions and no easy answers.

I learned to practice harm reduction without knowing that such a philosophy existed.

Harm reduction is a diverse set of strategies that were "designed to reduce the harmful consequences"[1] of drug use but have been

143

used successfully working with individuals who trade sex. They are not so much a list of things to do but rather a list of guiding principles to follow. Ultimately, the principles are guided by one overarching rule: individuals are to be treated as adult agents in their own lives and with respect.

HIPS (Helping Individual Prostitutes Survive) is a pioneer organization in using the harm reduction model for serving sex workers. Their mission is "to assist female, male, and transgender individuals engaging in sex work in Washington, D.C., in leading healthy lives. Using a harm reduction model, HIPS' programs strive to address the impact that HIV/AIDS, sexually transmitted infections, discrimination, poverty, violence and drug use have on the lives of individuals engaging in sex work."[2]

Volunteers must become fluent in harm reduction. Harm reduction principles are incorporated into every sex worker interaction, including outreach. Nonjudgment is critical to every interaction. It's also particularly important to understand that harm reduction is a strategy that's employed, because it builds trust in relationships. But it's not an act–we don't "act" like we validate the sex worker–we actually validate her. We believe that all people have value, even the ones that society tells us do not.

The sex worker's feelings and perceptions are validated. This is not agreeing with everything a sex worker says to you. Instead, it's a communication tool–active listening. When an individual says something to you, you put it into your own words and say it back. She tells you that she's scared of an ex-boyfriend who knows that she's on the street tonight, and you say, "So your ex-boyfriend knowing where you are concerns you."

Being heard is the key component of this interaction. Some people go days without feeling like anyone has heard them. And given the "invisible" nature of people in poverty, often they feel like no one listens.

The sex worker is affirmed for her strengths. This may seem superficial, but much like feeling like no one listens, very few individuals point out positive traits of sex workers. And being in sex work requires a lot of strengths, no matter your disposition. It takes good people-reading skills to be a sex worker. Working on the streets, on the phones, in strip clubs, or off the Internet takes courage. Most of the sex workers I've met are intelligent. And frequently, they are warm, friendly, fun, and funny.

No sex worker ever needs to hear derogatory things about themselves or the work they do. As individuals, we all understand what our limitations are, what we're doing in our lives that goes against societal norms, and how we put ourselves at risk. Rest assured that the internal critic is taking care of making sure that the sex worker feels shame and guilt about the work she is doing.

Being a part of the sex trade does not fully identify any individual any more than being a lawyer, garbage worker, or astronaut defines a person. Each of us has full lives apart from the work we do. It is perfectly acceptable to show interest and curiosity about aspects of the sex worker's life apart from her work in recognition that she is a whole person and that her job doesn't define her.

The relationship between a case worker, a volunteer for an organization, or an outreach worker and a sex worker is not equal. The person with something to give has more power in the relationship than the person who is in need. Note that the relationship is not equal, but the people certainly are equal.

Due in part to the unequal relationship, sex workers will tell case workers and volunteers what they want to hear. They will, even though they do not have a problem with being a sex worker, say to you, "I know sex work is bad." This is often because they want something from you, so they want to tell you what they perceive you want to hear. One way to wade through this is to say something unexpected. While a sex worker will expect you to be negative about sex work, say something positive about the work . . . normalize their experience. For instance, "I know trading sex is difficult, but it is better than owing someone else for the things you need."

Many of the women I know who worked in strip clubs and online escorting have decided to trade sex because of their fierce dedication to paying their own way. It is a determination to support themselves, to not owe anyone anything, to not be dependent on anyone else that leads them into sex work. Sometimes sex work is the best money they can make with limited resources and limited education.

In any given interaction with a sex worker, once she opens up, it's good to take an opportunity to talk about risk reduction. The first step is to identify risks that exist for the sex worker. Here's a good example of doing this while giving out condoms.

Volunteer: I see that you need a lot of condoms and that you prefer the Magnums. Why do you like these?
SW: I prefer the Magnums because the guys I date always say they need them for the size.
Volunteer: Is it difficult to get men to wear the condoms?

SW: Of course it is. I wish there was a way for me to put it on instead of them.

Volunteer: Have you ever thought about putting it on with your mouth? If it's done in a way that men seem to enjoy, then there's not so much negotiating about it.

SW: I could do that? Show me how!

The risk that we identified was not always using a condom (although we never said it aloud). We were trying to identify ways to make sure to use a condom every time. We gave an easier way to negotiate condom wearing because it makes it more likely.

There are a lot of risks that can be identified, too many to do an exhaustive list, but they can include HIV transmission, violence, arrest, drug use and overuse, and sexually transmitted infections (STIs). Having to face any one of these obstacles adds sometimes insurmountable disadvantages to an already difficult life.

For instance, consider a sex worker who has a record of arrest for prostitution. Police officers, judges, attorneys, and social workers think that arresting sex workers will lead them to getting out of sex work. However, the opposite is often true. An arrest and conviction can actually trap a person in sex work. Many corporations today require a police clearance and a background check. If a sex worker has been arrested for prostitution, how likely is she to apply for a position that requires a background check?

In a longer-term relationship, the volunteer should notice and reinforce progress toward better self-care. Oftentimes, this will be affirming things that will conflict with the all-or-nothing nature of the "drug addiction as a disease" model. But harm reduction honors small steps to change. Affirming someone who is cutting down on heroin by using marijuana may seem odd at first, but it begins to come naturally.

Over time, the people you see each week or month will begin to trust you. They'll be excited when you visit. If they're in a drop-in center, they'll tell you more about their lives, little by little. They'll begin to trust you. This is a really important part of this caring work. In strip clubs and on the stroll, there are signs that people are beginning to trust you.

The first time I knew a strip club in Birmingham was beginning to trust our team was when we visited the club on Valentine's Day and the house mom had a big basket of candy for us. Their hospitality was a sign that the club had some confidence in us. There are other ways that people have shared trust. Club owners have given us donations. Dancers have brought over their new friends, saying, "You can really trust these women." Escorts have shared very personal stories about abuse, arrest, and family issues.

One of the biggest moments of trust at HIPS came when a regular participant knocked on my door to ask, "Would you give me an HIV test?" He was very high risk, as he was an MSM (a man who has sex with men, as the Center for Disease Control designates). And he had traded sex for several years. In his midforties, he was grateful to have the test with people who he trusted.

His test came back positive. He was prepared for it, though, and was ready to seek treatment. But he wanted to find out his status from people that he trusted who would still love him when they knew the truth.

This is why trust and trustworthiness is so important. Volunteers, case managers, social workers, and ministers don't bring about change in people's lives. People have to instigate change in their own lives. But if we are worthy of trust, sometimes we get invited along to witness, support, care, and accompany our friends in their lives.

Survival in the sex industry requires a couple of skills that can get in the way of building relationships with sex workers. The first skill is suspicion. Suspicion keeps you safe, it keeps bad people at bay, and it guards your emotional health, too.

The second skill is manipulation. Manipulation is the art of getting what you want and need by using flattery, indignation, sexual desire, or any other means necessary. You have to understand that manipulation is second nature to many sex workers. However, it is not always negative. And it is not always obvious. But working with individuals in the sex industry, you have to be aware that manipulation is not only possible; it's probable.

Being aware of manipulation is the key to avoiding it and to modeling open and transparent conversation. Manipulation reminds me of a hook, like the claw machine from the carnival. The manipulator is trying to land a stuffed animal from your heart. The claw goes down, lands on a stuffed animal, and begins to bring it up. It's up to you to slide out of the manipulation. If a manipulator finds that a certain hook won't work, rest assured that she will try another hook.

What are common hooks? Pity, injustice, children, hunger, youth, desire, anger, you name it. Any emotion can be used as a hook. It just has to be the one that works on you. That's why it's important to understand, in working with people in a position where you have power and possessions and they don't, that you control your emotional response.

There are a couple of key phrases to look for to indicate that someone may be practicing manipulation. One key indicator of manipulation is being unwilling to take no for an answer. A "no" will be met with all different types of resistance and argument. Think about a time someone tried to convince you of something you didn't believe. They probably cajoled, argued, begged, yelled, dug their heels in, and even tried reverse psychology.

That kind of manipulation is easy to see. There are other hooks that are more difficult to pinpoint. There's the "it's not me, it's you!" hook. This hook removes the responsibility for a person's actions to the other person in the conflict. Another is shifting blame: "It's not me, it's someone else! They're doing it to me!" The goal here is to shift the conflict from the two individuals involved and add another person to take the heat. Another tactic is silence. Sometimes in conversation, someone will use the manipulative tool of totally changing the subject—the manipulator leaves his or her mark in confusion.

Another way to tell someone is practicing manipulation is in how they try to sell a person something they don't want. They say, "This could be your last chance," trying to get a quick response. They sometimes threaten loss if their target doesn't comply, maybe saying, "Do with it what you will, it's your funeral."

One of the best manipulations to move someone to our team is to gossip about someone else. In the extreme, this is known as triangulation. If there are three people in a triangle, pushing one corner away pulls the other two corners closer. A sentence like, "Can you believe what such-and-such is doing?" can be an effective manipulation tool.

Another tool is guilt, where the manipulator may say, "My life depends on you." One of the key things to understand about sex workers is they are survivors. When you know this, you can better gauge someone's sincerity. Except under the threat of extreme violence, a sex worker's daily needs will most likely be met. So the urgency, even emergency, of some needs has to be evaluated.

I worked with a participant at HIPS, a trans woman who was living in a homeless shelter. In Washington, D.C., it is the law that trans individuals be given the option of which gender-based housing options they prefer. So she was housed with women. However, there had been some issues with her. She had been discovered masturbating in the common restroom by another resident. The other women were uncomfortable with her in using the bathrooms at the same time, so she was given a schedule for the restroom.

It was a hostile environment for her. We had worked up some options for housing for her, but any of the available transition homes required thirty days of sobriety for her to move in. She didn't want to remain sober for that long.

She had indicated that she wanted another option for housing, but for what she was willing to do, a shelter was the only one we could identify.

At 10:00 p.m. on a Friday, she called the HIPS hotline to say that she needed a place to stay the night. We had funds to help folks in crisis with a hotel, so we looked into her story. The hotline volunteer called me. The participant said that she had been put out of her sister's house. She was desperate when she talked with the client advocate. Finally, I instructed the volunteer, "Ask her where she is."

Turns out she was in the shelter. She just didn't want to be there. And longer-term housing was out because she didn't want to meet their requirements. And there was nothing that could be done about her longer-term needs anyway, since it was late Friday night! So we let her deal with the consequences of her choices.

To do this, you must be disconnected emotionally from situations. Emotional disconnection is not the same thing as not caring or not being emotionally available to a participant. It's just that we don't respond to the situation or connect from our emotions, like fear or panic (the feelings we would have if we were on the streets for a night). If the volunteer or client advocate had overidentified with the woman, HIPS would have rushed in to meet those needs. Instead, we mediated our emotional response, which is best for the participant.

Why? Because meeting real needs is better than meeting felt needs. Real needs are air, water, food, clothing, and shelter. And these are needed every day. Real needs are long term. *Until these needs are met in a sustainable way, all the other needs are secondary.* Felt needs are extras. Cigarettes, drugs, a bed with a pillow, and a car are all secondary needs. It's important to meet these needs, but they are not emergency needs. And if the real needs are met, these secondary needs begin to come to the forefront.

Harm reduction recognizes that the sex industry is real and affects real and complex individuals and works to minimize harmful effects, not ignore or condemn them. Looking back at Jesus' response to the woman at the well, harm reduction doesn't believe that the circumstances that lead some into the sex industry are monolithic or black and white. It isn't a Pollyanna view of sex work. It takes into account that there is potential and actual harm that comes from sex work. Harm reductionists respect those differences and try to meet the individual precisely where she is, understanding that there's no cookie-cutter fix to anyone's life.

This approach requires that services and resources provided to individuals who trade sex must be nonjudgmental and noncoercive and must be based on the needs and wants of that individual. Why is this? It is because no change really happens without the subject's participation. Treatment for drug and alcohol use can be a great thing—but it's worthless if the drug user doesn't want to be there.

A critical feature of this work is making sure that individuals who have experience in the sex industry are the ones who create and serve in the programs designed to serve them. A successful program will be *for* sex workers and *by* sex workers. Even if sex workers aren't the primary agents in an organization, it is imperative that sex workers be a part of the process in deciding not only what is important but also the manner in which things will be done.

Harm reduction sees individuals who trade sex as the primary agents in deciding their futures and seeks to empower them by sharing information and supporting strategies and resources that meet their actual needs. Recognizing agency and not treating individuals as victims is very important. Victims don't have agency. Survivors do.

An effective ally must magnify the choices and agency of those involved in the sex industry, many times acting as an intermediary speaking for sex workers when it's not safe for sex workers but always striving for them to speak with their own voices. He or she makes known the choices and the agency of individuals who trade sex. He or she doesn't "speak for" sex workers when it is more appropriate for sex workers to speak.

Sometimes harm reduction seems like a tactic, sometimes it seems little more than semantics. But it's not. It's based on a very basic respect for human beings, a respect that every individual has the right to live his or her life in the manner that he or she wants as long as it doesn't infringe on the rights of others. It is the same as seeing God in the other person. It is recognition that this person deserves all the rights and privileges that come with being a child of God and created in the image of God. Individuals can and should be held responsible for their own decisions and honored for those same decisions, afforded the rights, responsibilities, and opportunities to make their lives better.

Is it too much to ask?

Among all the discussions between sex workers and academics, religious folks and advocates, it seems as if everyone is looking for a one-size-fits-all solution to the entire sex industry. I believe there is one solution that works for every person in sex work and that is acceptance and advocacy for increasing personal choice. But it has to be personalized to each person. That is what increasing agency is all about.

Using this approach of increasing agency in all areas will change everybody's life—from the CEO to the guru to the office worker to the stay-at-home mom. Our lives are made better by increasing the number of options we have for happiness. And we increase agency through education, work opportunities, belief in ourselves, reduction in prejudice and stigma, and having friends and family who are close.

If you treat all people in sex work as if they have no agency, you become no different from traffickers making choices for the people in sex work. In effect, you take away any agency that they have. On the other hand, if you treat all people in sex work as if they have full agency, you don't do enough to protect those who have no agency. You leave them enslaved.

Bottom line: if you or your organization wants to impact the lives of sex workers, you must find ways to increase agency for people who are trading sex.

So what are some practical ways to do that?

Support groups are a great way to increase agency because people who have been isolated are able to tell their stories without judgment. They also enable peer education—sex workers can learn tips to make their own work safer and more productive.

Classes can be another good way to increase agency, teaching particular skills such as budgeting, resumé writing, interviewing, sales, costume making, and negotiation. I can imagine all these being good skills for sex workers. From my own experience, informational classes are a tough sell. Who wants to spend an hour learning how to budget? I'd rather sleep.

Organized events with rituals are very important in the sex worker community and certainly increase agency. On the December 17, 2009, march in Washington, D.C., in honor of the International Day to End Violence against Sex Workers, we had a "die-in." The marchers lay on the ground to signify the death of sex workers around the world. After reading the names of the sex workers who had been killed in the last year, people took the microphone and told their stories of loss and violence. It was a powerful ritual.

Vigils and protests definitely lead to increased agency. Part of the reason they work so well is that the protesters find they're not alone. It fights isolation. But it is also a moment to tell stories in a safe place.

Offering health services for sex workers can become very empowering. Imagine sitting in a doctor's office when he asks you about your sexual history. If you're a sex worker, what are you likely to share? Do you tell the truth? What if the doctor is used to seeing sex workers and has been trained specially to deal with issues of sex work? What if she can give you tips to keep safe and to protect your tender spots from the wear and tear? How much more likely are you to tell the truth?

Helping individuals manage their health is an agency-building process. It can often seem like an uphill battle, but being able to make decisions about your health, finding a doctor who is respectful and knowledgeable, and knowing precisely how your health is gives you the opportunities to be more in control of your life and body.

On that note, exercise classes are a great way to build agency. Exercise offers the health benefits of feeling stronger, releasing endorphins, relieving stress, and increasing flexibility. As I mentioned, when I first started Star Light, we had a great yoga class for about a year. The dancers loved it, and it was great not only for flexibility but also for relationship building.

The Red Umbrella Project (http://www.redumbrellaproject. org) offers classes on storytelling and media making that benefit the agency of sex workers. Learning to tell their stories in an effective way helps to change public perception of sex workers and combats the stigma and isolation sex workers feel. It's also a great way to advocate for the rights of sex workers.

There are hundreds of other ways to build agency. The way you offer agency will match your personality and will provide what's most needed in your community.

The first step in determining *how* to work with sex workers is performing a formal needs assessment. Without this, you might as well hang up your hat and move along. Assessing real needs is the most important step in determining what the needs of the sex workers in your community are, how those needs meet up with the skills and objectives of your volunteers, and what you can do to match those.

It can start with Internet research. What are the strip clubs in your town? Where are the strolls in your neighborhoods (where sex workers offer their services on the street)? If there are sex workers online in your town, how many do you see? At this stage of the process, it's nearly impossible to talk with a sex worker–she's not going to trust you–so you're going to have to rely on what you can gather through research, not conversation.

You should also begin to investigate sex worker–specific resources in your town. Is there an organization doing outreach? What about the courts? Is there a diversion program or a John school? Are there HIV prevention programs that are working with sex workers? Or are there antitrafficking groups? Sometimes antitrafficking groups have drop-in centers, and although your approaches and goals may be different, they can be great places to gather information. Especially keep an eye out for resources created *by* sex workers. Resources created by sex workers are the number one approach to effective sex worker outreach!

Who knows best what a sex worker needs? Even after the best needs assessment ever, if you weren't a sex worker, you will never know what she really needs. But if you find a well-run (or even not particularly well-run) project, created for and by sex workers, you should immediately call them and ask them how they can use your expertise. Because chances are they're doing the work that needs to be done.

You may have to build trust with them. If they tell you their major initiative is to provide a potluck for sex workers, ask, "Can I bring your snacks every week?" If they're advocating for decriminalization in their area, then say, "How can I get the word out?" If they offer court support to sex workers who have been arrested, say, "Can I help pay [or raise funds to pay] transportation costs, court costs, or fees?"

When I first started Star Light, there was a reporter from a local newspaper who wanted to interview me about the work we were doing. I went into the conversation with the reporter with fear and trepidation. Could I be interviewed about the specific work I was doing with sex workers in town without using the sex workers to promote my agenda?

Ultimately, I decided that I could not promote the organization without exploiting individuals in sex work, especially when the reporter asked me to pose for pictures in one of my favorite clubs. A couple of weeks after saying no, I was visiting the club on our monthly visit. But I forgot a special gift for a dancer in my car that was a few miles' drive away. I had no idea whether she would be at the club that day, but I felt, deep inside (OK, it was the Holy Spirit) that it would be important to return for the gift.

When we returned to the club, I was met with the manager telling me that this same reporter had come around to the club twenty minutes earlier—just when I would've arrived. The manager made it very clear that he did not want me talking to the reporter and somehow that put me and the manager on the same team. Since I was there for the dancers, having the manager accept me and welcome our volunteers was important. I supported his point of view, so he supported the work I was doing.

Support the work the former sex workers are already doing. Likely, that's the right work in your area to do. SWOP (Sex Workers Outreach Project) "is a national social justice network dedicated to the fundamental human rights of sex workers and their communities, focusing on ending violence and stigma through education and advocacy."[3] Created by sex workers for sex workers, this organization has sites throughout the United States and is an advocacy group for sex worker's rights. They have a resource page for local sites. You can start there.

What about other resources? You will need poverty resources, including food banks, clothing closets, homeless shelters, domestic violence shelters, health services, and mental health services. Are any of these resources seeing sex workers? Don't be afraid to be blunt about it. Social service organizations like all the help they can get.

Once you've decided to reach out to sex workers and think you want to start a project, what's one of the first things you need? Here's where it all comes back to money. Of all the challenges of working with individuals who trade sex, finding the money to do it is the most difficult.

Every organization I know of that treats sex workers as agents in their own lives or that uses a harm reduction model ends up having difficulty raising capital. Anyone who refuses to talk about outreach without using victim language and imagery is likely to have serious financial issues. Why? Because raising money for individuals perceived as full agents in their lives means they've simply made bad decisions in most people's eyes. Donors want to give money to victims, and innocent victims, if possible.

Some organizations have had success fundraising around HIV prevention. They have received money to do HIV testing, peer education, needle exchange, and condom distribution. However, HIV funding is drying up. Whether it's from the economy or from the changes in HIV/AIDS treatment, organizations won't likely be able to rely on HIV/AIDS funds.

I spoke with a gentleman who works at the Department of Health in Washington, D.C., and he said, "Many of us have worked our whole lives in HIV prevention. I've been here since the late eighties when everyone said this was a gay disease. But many of us will have to find new jobs now." He went on to tell me that when he meets a young person who wants to go into HIV prevention work, he says, "Find something different!" Simply, it's not needed anymore.

Gone are the days when you could depend on the church to meet your needs. With church budgets being swallowed by building costs, the aging of the local congregation, and the way donors give money differently, there's just not much money for outreach. Even if churches are willing to give money in direct aid to your population, they are generally unwilling to pay salaries.

Unfortunately, what many people who care about unpopular groups of people have to do is either work a side job or do without things like paid holidays, fancy nights out, and health insurance. Or they have to compromise their beliefs.

Still others beg in a way that can feel like compromise. I do have friends who write fundraising letters that talk about the way they suffer as people who don't have enough money to live, much less do the work they set out to do. I empathize. Certainly. But these are still choices you are making, and the people you work with have much less than you.

If you are living in poverty to work with individuals in sex work, people without homes, or sexual assault and domestic abuse survivors, the best thing I can tell you is the work is *important*. And poverty will help you understand the issues many sex workers face every day. In some way, it's important to survive this. On the other hand, it stinks. Because of that, it makes self-care all the more important.

The organizations that do have a lot of money are the antitrafficking organizations. And perhaps if you really want to do this work, you can go through an antitrafficking organization and spend enough time there to either change their culture or build a job that you would be proud of. On the other hand, it might give you enough of an education to accept that there's no easy answers to increasing agency for others.

I've never been very good at compromise. Nor have I had much luck in having different messages to different groups of people. Some have one message for donors and another for their clients. This feels too disjointed to me. I don't want to produce a letter, a blog post, or give a sermon or speech I would feel uncomfortable giving if a sex worker was in the audience.

Star Light was very successful in reaching out to people in sex work, but we never raised enough money to do more than pay simple expenses. There was never enough money for salaries, an office space, or a large marketing budget. People really don't care about sex workers. And if you do, you will probably have to find a different way to subsidize this passion—or be independently wealthy.

At this point in your research, you should be getting an idea of where the concentration of sex workers are working and the resources that are available to them. Now is the time to start thinking about building relationships.

If the sex workers are in a strip club, then visiting the club might be best. If your town has a lot of street-level sex workers, then going out on the stroll with some hospitality could be great—hot chocolate on a cold night is a wonderful thing! Once you build the relationships, then comes the time to begin building a program.

The bottom line is to listen more than you talk.

After listening, you will probably find a way to do outreach. Why is outreach necessary? Because sex workers aren't going to come find you. It's as easy as that. When you're in sex work and you go looking for help or for resources, you are more likely to get the door slammed in your face or be shamed by some "well-meaning" person than you are to find help or resources. And it only takes a time or two to figure out that people aren't going to help but hurt with judgment and condescension.

Go online, advocate for them publicly, visit strip clubs, or find the evening strolls. It means going out of your way to make sure that sex workers know they are cared about.

I used to think you had to have something to offer off the stroll in order to meet someone on the stroll. I'm not sure if that's necessary anymore. But you should have something to give if you're visiting a club or on the stroll. Even if you don't have an organized ministry with an office, a Web site, and a phone number, you can make a difference in an evening.

In order to understand sex work, you should approach it as if you are learning a new culture. What is the culture like? Is there a hierarchy? Is there someone who acts as a gatekeeper? Is there someone who has to give permission for the sex workers to interact with you?

In strip clubs, there is a hierarchy. There's a bouncer or a door person who is the gatekeeper. There's a manager who should give you permission to interact with the dancers. There's usually a house-mom who can help in getting to know the dancers. If she thinks you're safe, the dancers will often think you are safe, too.

Every club and stroll has its own language and hospitality, too. Sexual language is common, especially lingo that you may not understand. Do not feel self-conscious about asking for explanations. There are drug references, too. If you do feel uncomfortable asking, remember it and ask someone else when you leave the club.

There is a "morality" to every club and stroll, too, an ethical code that the sex workers live by. It may seem odd or different from your code. For example, I had a dancer tell me that she "wasn't like those women over there. They date the men." "Date" is a euphemism for having sex for money. One escort may not kiss. Another may not do oral sex. Another may not do anal. Sometimes sex workers use judgment about those acts to distance themselves from other sex workers. The best approach is to ignore those statements or treat them head on. I might say something like, "I'm sure she has her reasons [for not kissing]," or "Somebody's got to do it [anal], right?"

What are the criteria for being someone who does outreach? The most important one is to really care and want to make a difference in the lives of sex workers. The second is being accepting. The third is a commitment to be compassionate and to do better at every turn. Constantly working to be more accepting is really important.

One thing that happens in clubs and on the stroll is that they are pounded with "Christians" who are telling them how they should change their lives. A club we were visiting in Richmond had picketers/Christians yelling at them nightly. There were a dozen or so men outside the club yelling at the dancers as they entered work. The weather was severely cold, so one of the evenings they were there, the bartender sent out hot chocolate to the protesters.

The Christian protesters quit coming soon after that.

There are different groups that visit the clubs to evangelize the individuals working in the clubs. Some groups infiltrate the clubs, not saying exactly who they are, and leave pamphlets. Club employees understandably get upset with these groups.

If you're going into a club or on the stroll and you talk about being Christian, you'll have to deal with the baggage that these judgmental people have left. The easiest way to do that is to face it head on. You can say, "I'm sorry that happened. Sometimes Christians are jerks. I will do my best not to be a jerk."

If you are visiting a strip club, try to visit at a less busy time and be sure to pay a cover, if asked. You should be paying like any other customer. Paying for the services you receive is a sign of respect for their business.

One person in your group should take a moment to speak to the manager, explaining why you are visiting, offering an opportunity to the working women to talk with you. If your group has brought in gifts or condoms, be sure to mention them to the bouncer and to the manager. The manager has the ability to make or break you in club visits, and it is a good idea to remember his name.

When you pick a table, it is a good idea to be away from the stage areas, if possible. Remember that these women are working, and you are an interruption in their day, just as if someone were visiting your office. Allow them the opportunity to approach you rather than you approaching them.

Strip clubs are very unusual places, and being on the stroll in the evening can be very disconcerting. Even though we've seen it in the movies, the reality is very different than we expect. Our expectations do not always match the real thing. The first visit is the most difficult because there is no way to be completely prepared. But there are some things you can expect.

First, expect to be surprised at the level of sexuality. My first assumption was that the sexuality would not be all that evident because I think about the club as a money-making venture, not a sex venture. Not true! It's definitely a sex venture. There's a lot of joking and talk about sex. Get over it! Flirting is a way that folks on the stroll understand talking with people, so don't be surprised if someone flirts with you.

Second, expect to be surprised at the level of camaraderie between the sex workers. During the first dance in a club, all the dancers and customers surround the new girl and affirm her beauty, her performance, and her talent. This first dance is their initiation and can be the most money they ever make in one dance. This dance is meant to make the dancer feel comfortable and confident.

There is usually one woman that protects and teaches a new woman. That protective one will generally become her first friend in the club and will remain close throughout their working relationship.

Third, don't expect the sex workers to say bad things about their customers. They have relationships with their clients. The natural outcome of this is that the women have relationships with the men, and they come to enjoy those relationships.

Please don't be surprised if you find women in sex work who are professing Christians. On a friend's first visit to a club, one of the women was so excited to see her! The dancer said, "I have been praying that someone would come!" A large proportion of the women will be Christian, especially in the South, where growing up Christian is the norm.

Outreach has a different effect on each person who participates. Frankly, a common response is anger. Women have walked away angry with men who perpetuate sexually oriented businesses. The first thing that I noticed after my first visit was a deep restlessness. Others have had extreme sadness. What will your response be? It varies from person to person, and it varies from visit to visit. So be prepared for anything. Be sure to have people available to hang out with you after the visit.

Your group should do a debriefing following the visit and you should talk about your feelings if you can. If you can't talk that quickly, then be sure to keep in contact after your visit. You will need time to process.

In *The Wisdom of Whores: Bureaucrats, Brothels, and the Business of AIDS*, Elizabeth Pisani concludes the book with a couple of statements. She says that the problem surrounding HIV is that adults get HIV by having unprotected sex and/or sharing needles while injecting drugs; that they pass the virus on when they have a high viral load in their blood (early in the infection or due to another infection); and that HIV is transmitted most easily when it comes into contact with sores, lesions, or a foreskin. Therefore, the solution is to reduce the exchange "of body fluids between infected and unin- fected people," reduce the viral load in those with HIV, and "close all potential 'open doors' so the virus can't get into the uninfected person."[4]

It's a straightforward solution to HIV, but why hasn't it been implemented? She says that the *who* (sex workers, drug injectors, men who have sex with men, trans women, and people in prison) and the *what* (reduce exchange of body fluids, reduce viral load, close doors of infection) are the same no matter where you are in the world.

But what's different is the *how*. How you ensure that sex workers will use condoms in Haiti will be different from how you ensure sex workers in China use condoms. How you get clean needles distributed in Canada will be different than distributing them in South Africa.

In order to really make a difference to a community, you have to understand their particular context.

I can tell you who sex workers are, how they got to where they are, what sex workers, in large part, need to thrive, and the basics of building relationships.

But what I cannot tell you is *how* this can be done in your community.

A few years ago, Star Light had a team of volunteers who visited a strip club in Atlanta. The club had a mix of Eastern Europeans and Americans. There were some African Americans and some whites. The clientele was a mix of Latino, African American, and preppy white boys.

The team visited the club once or twice a month for over a year. Some days, they'd be really well received. Other days, it would be like no one had ever seen them before. They always struggled with how to meet the folks, in the colloquial words of outreach groups, "where they are at," and how to best meet their needs.

I received a call one night as the team was scheduled to visit their club. The leader said to me, "The club is closed tonight, and the manager is telling us that the dancers aren't there. Should we reschedule?" Mind you, this club was in the community where these volunteers lived, and I was seven hundred miles away. "What do you think you should do?" I asked.

She answered, "I think we should try again tomorrow."

Once you spend time listening and observing, you will understand the context of the sex work you're seeing, whether it's online, in person at a strip club, or in a church. And that's where intuition comes in.

When I was training volunteers, the most difficult part of training them was to have them trust their own intuition. You can call it intuition or you can call it the Holy Spirit, but it feels the same. It's a feeling in the middle of your being that says "Do this" or "Don't do that."

In the end, it really is all about learning to listen.

*     *     *

The manager of the dancers at a club met me at the door one day when I was visiting. "Where have you been?" she asked. When I asked what was happening, she told me about a dancer from the club who had given birth to a premature baby who had died in her arms. Without health insurance or a savings plan, she was facing months of not working and needed help. She had moved into a new apartment, had no furniture, and was worried about making rent.

So my Star Light team got to work. We identified a ministry for people who had been through a fire, and they agreed to give us a whole household of furniture, from sofas and beds to ice trays and linens. We borrowed a truck and got it all. The housemom met me at the young woman's apartment, and we unloaded the furniture and set up her new home. In addition, we found a church with an emergency rent program and paid her rent for two months. The dancer was worried that the furniture would be ugly, but I paid special attention to her Betty Page hairdo and picked 1940s furniture with flair.

Several months later, our team visited the club again. Just as we were about to leave the club, the DJ announced that the young woman was going on stage and that her dance was dedicated to "the church ladies." She got up and danced to the song *Your Own Personal Jesus* by Depeche Mode. They sang about someone who cares and someone who shares. Don't we all need a personal Jesus sometimes?

# Notes

## Tamar's Story

[1] Leah Abramowitz, *Tales of Nehama: Impressions of the Life and Teaching of Nehama Leibowitz* (Jerusalem: Gefen Publishing House, 2003), 147.

[2] Ibid.

## Chapter 1: Girls, Girls, Girls

[1] Maureen Dowd, "What Tina Wants," *Vanity Fair*, January 2009, http://www.vanityfair.com/magazine/2009/01/tina_fey200901.

[2] Tina Fey, *Bossypants* (New York: Reagan Arthur Books, 2011), 220.

[3] Chris Rock, *Chris Rock: Never Scared* (HBO special), aired April 17, 2004 (Burbank, CA: HBO, 2004), DVD, clip accessed February 2, 2012, http://www.youtube.com/watch?v=tojBadSr2zI.

[4] "¡Qué Sorpresa!" originally aired February 11, 2011, *30 Rock*, season 5, episode 13, aired February 11, 2011.

[5] "Sensitive Language Guide: The Victim, The Survivor," Women's Funding Network, accessed May 27, 2011, www.womensfundingnetwork.org, http://www.womensfundingnetwork.org/AFNAP-toolkit/sensitive-language-guide/victim-survivor.

[6] Stepping Stones is a Canadian nonprofit that reaches out to sex workers. Their Web site and these ads can be found at http://steppingstonesns.ca.

## Chapter 3: Pour Some Sugar on Me

[1] Brian Fikkert and Steven Corbett, *When Helping Hurts: Alleviating Poverty without Hurting the Poor . . . and Yourself* (Chicago: Moody, 2009), 71.

[2] "Statistical Abstract of the United States: 2012," U.S. Census Bureau, accessed February 2, 2011, http://www.census.gov/compendia/statab/2012/tables/12s0709.pdf.

[3] "Income, Poverty, and Health Insurance Coverage in the United States: 2009," U.S. Census Bureau, accessed February 2, 2011 2010, http://www.census.gov.

[4] Melissa Petro, "Thoughts from a Former Craigslist Sex Worker," Huffington Post, September 7, 2010, accessed February 5, 2011, http://www.huffingtonpost.com/melissa-petro/post_803_b_707975.html.

## Chapter 4: R-E-S-P-E-C-T

[1] "Member Search," Black Americans in Congress, accessed September 13, 2011, http://baic.house.gov/member-profiles.

[2] "Prison Inmates at Midyear 2009–Statistical Tables," U.S. Department of Justice, accessed February 29, 2012, http://bjs.ojp.usdoj.gov/content/pub/pdf/pim09st.pdf.

[3] "Fortune 500 Women CEOs," CNNMoney, accessed February 29, 2012, http://money.cnn.com/magazines/fortune/fortune500/2011/womenceos.

[4] Jennifer Kiel, "Women, the Recession, and the Impending Economic Recovery," *Graziadio Business Review* 12, no. 4 (2009), accessed February 26, 2012, http://gbr.pepperdine.edu/2010/08/women-the-recession-and-the-impending-economic-recovery/~.

[5] "Modest Recovery Largely Leaves Women Behind," National Women's Law Center, accessed February 29, 2012, http://www.nwlc.org/resource/modest-recovery-largely-leaves-women-behind.

[6] Jeff Hayes and Heidi Hartmann, "Women and Men Living on the Edge: Economic Insecurity after the Great Recession," Institute for Women's Policy Research, accessed February 29, 2012, http://www.iwpr.org/publications/pubs/women-and-men-living-on-the-edge-economic-insecurity-after-the-great-recession.

[7] "Who Are the Victims? Breakdown by Gender and Age," Rape, Abuse, and Incest National Network (RAINN), accessed February 26, 2012, http://www.rainn.org/get-information/statistics/sexual-assault-victims.

[8] Ibid.

[9] Ibid.

[10] "Myths and Facts about Mental Illness," National Center on Workforce and Disability, accessed on February 26, 2012, http://www.onestops.info/article.php?article_id=62.

[11] Seth Godin, *Linchpin: Are You Indispensable?* (New York: Penguin, 2010), 16.

[12] Brooke, "Life Is Beautiful," Star Light Ministries, Inc., accessed August 27, 2011, http://starlight-ministries.org/wp_blog_1/?p=184.

[13] "What Is Intersex?" Intersex Society of North America, accessed August 28, 2011, http://www.isna.org/faq/what_is_intersex.

[14] Jaime M. Grant, Lisa A. Mottet, Justin Tanis, Jack Harrison, Jody L. Herman, and Mara Keisling, "Injustice at Every Turn: A Report of the National Transgender Discrimination Survey," accessed March 22, 2011, http://www.thetaskforce.org/reports_and_research/ntds.

[15] Trafficking in Persons Report, 10th Edition," June 2010, U.S. State Department, 8, accessed February 29, 2012, www.state.gov/documents/organization/142979.pdf.

[16] In most states, a court order is required to change your gender. Court orders cost money. If you get pulled over by a police officer who looks at your identification and finds that it doesn't match your appearance, you'll have some explaining to do. Same issue if you're seeking employment. Your birth certificate will need changing, too.

Of individuals who have changed gender, only 21 percent have been able to change all their legal documents to their new gender. About half have been able to change their driver's licenses, and 40 percent indicate the mismatch in gender has resulted in harassment and verbal assault.

And while proper identification may seem like a small thing, it's not small in North America, where we're reliant upon our credit ratings and identification for housing, utilities, banking, telephones, and Internet service.

One-fifth of transgender or gender nonconforming people report being homeless at some point in their lives because of their gender identity. When those same individuals sought housing in a homeless shelter, 55 percent of them reported discrimination. Twenty-nine percent of them were turned away completely and 22 percent report being sexually assaulted by staff or other residents.

Discrimination in housing makes it really tough to be off the streets. Nearly a quarter of the people who responded to the survey indicated they have been harassed by the police. Sixty percent of African American trans men and women have reported being harassed and physically or sexually assaulted by the police.

## Chapter 5: You Shook Me All Night Long

[1] There is no biblical evidence that Mary Magdalene engaged in prostitution. The work of Pope Gregory I (ca. 540–604 CE) is the first extant writing to equate Mary Magdalene with the "sinful woman" of Luke 7:37, who anoints Jesus from her alabaster jar.

[2] Melissa Farley, "Prostitution and the Invisibility of Harm," *Women & Therapy* 26, nos. 3–4 (2003): 247–80, accessed September 11, 2011, http://www.prostitution research.com/how_prostitution_works/000176.html.

[3] Luisa Kroll, "The World's Richest Self-Made Women," Forbes.com, June 14, 2010, accessed April 14, 2011, http://www.forbes.com/2010/06/14/richest-women -entrepreneur-billionaire-whitman-oprah-rowling.html.

## Chapter 6: Crazy Train

[1] *Urban Dictionary*, s.v. "Punter," accessed September 9, 2011, http://www.urban dictionary.com/define.php?term=punter.

[2] Amanda Hess, "The Secret Prostitution Code and What It Says about Johns," *Washington City Paper*, October 27, 2009, accessed September 9, 2011, http://www .washingtoncitypaper.com/blogs/sexist/2009/10/27/the-secret-prostitution -code-of-johns.

[3] Alex Johnson, "A Consumer Guide to Prostitutes Is Just a Click Away," MSNBC. com, accessed September 13, 2011, http://www.msnbc.msn.com/id/10879309/ns/ technology_and_science-tech_and_gadgets/t/consumer-guide-prostitutes-click-away.

[4] Melissa Farley, Emily Schuckman, Jacqueline M. Golding, Kristen Houser, Laura Jarrett, Peter Qualliotine, and Michele Decker, "Comparing Sex Buyers with Men Who Don't Buy Sex: 'You can have a good time with the servitude' vs. 'You're supporting a system of degradation'" Paper presented at Psychologists for Social Responsibility Annual Meeting July 15, 2011, Boston, accessed February 29, 2012, http://www.prostitutionresearch.com/c-prostitution-men-who-buy-sex.html.

[5] Aidan Wilcox, Kris Christmann, Michelle Rogerson, and Philip Birch, "Tack-ling the Demand for Prostitution: A Rapid Evidence Assessment of the Published Research Literature," University of Huttersfield, accessed September 9, 2011, http:// webarchive.nationalarchives.gov.uk/20100113210150/homeoffice.gov.uk/rds/ pdfs09/horr27c.pdf.

[6] Paul Debenedetto, "Former Sex Worker Teacher Resigns," NBC News, accessed September 10, 2011, http://www.nbcnewyork.com/news/Former-Sex -Worker-Teacher-Resigns-115773309.html.

## Chapter 7: Paradise City

[1] "Independent Contractor Defined," Internal Revenue Service, accessed Febru-ary 26, 2012, http://www.irs.gov/businesses/small/article/0,,id=179115,00.html.

[2] Lily Burana, *Strip City: A Stripper's Farewell Journey Across America.* (New York: Hyperion, 2001).

[3] Craig Seymour, *All I Could Bare: My Life in the Strip Clubs of Gay Washington, D.C.* (New York: Atria, 2009).

[4] Melissa Febos, *Whip Smart: A Memoir* (New York: Thomas Dunne, 2010).

[5] Ruth Fowler, *No Man's Land* (New York: Viking Penguin, 2008).

[6] Diablo Cody, *Candy Girl: A Year in the Life of an Unlikely Stripper* (New York: Gotham, 2006).

[7] David Henry Sterry and R. J. Martin Jr., editors, *Hos, Hookers, Call Girls, and Rent Boys: Professionals Writing on Life, Love, Money, and Sex* (Berkeley: Soft Skull, 2009).

[8] Priscilla Alexander and Frederique Delacoste, eds., *Sex Work: Writings by Women in the Sex Industry* (San Francisco: Cleis, 1998).

[9] The address for PornWikiLeaks was www.pornwikileaks.com, but as of February 29, 2012, this redirects to www.xxxfilmjobs.com. According to Wikipedia, PornWikiLeaks was shut down in July of 2011. "Porn WikiLeaks," Wikipedia, accessed February 29,2012, http://en.wikipedia.org/wiki/Porn_Wikileaks.

[10] "What Is Trafficking in Persons?" *Trafficking in Persons Report 2011*, U.S. Department of State, accessed February 29, 2012, http://www.state.gov/g/tip/rls/tiprpt/2011/164220.htm.

[11] "Trafficking in Persons Report, 10th Edition," June 2010, U.S. State Department, 8, accessed February 29, 2012, www.state.gov/documents/organization/142979.pdf.

[12] Manav Tanneeru, "The Challenges of Counting a 'Hidden Population,'" CNN Freedom Project, http://thecnnfreedomproject.blogs.cnn.com/2011/03/09/slavery-numbers/.

[13] Caroline Hames, Fleur Dewar, and Rebecca Napier-Moore, "Feeling Good about Feeling Bad: A Global Review of Evaluation in Anti-Trafficking Initiatives," Global Alliance against Trafficking in Women, 2010, August 31, 2011, accessed February 29, 2012, http://www.gaatw.org/publications/GAATW_Global_Review.FeelingGood.AboutFeelingBad.pdf.

[14] An *ABC World News* report said, "Of the 1.3 million jobs created in the last 12 months, some 90 percent have gone to men, according to a report from the Bureau of Labor Statistics." Bradley Blackburn, "Women Lag Behind Men in Economic Recovery," *ABC World News*, March 21, 2011, accessed February 29, 2012, http://abcnews.go.com/US/unemployment-recession-men-return-work-women-left-economic/story?id=13185406.

## Rahab's Story

[1] *Jewish Women: A Comprehensive Historical Encyclopedia*, s.v. "Rahab: Bible," by Tikva Frymer-Kensky, March 1, 2009, accessed August 26, 2011, http://jwa.org/encyclopedia/article/rahab-bible.

## Chapter 8: Roxanne

[1] Stewart Bishop, "Ex Prostitute Awarded $200,000 in Damages," Boston.com, March 16, 2011, accessed July 25, 2011, http://articles.boston.com/2011-03-16/news/29350054_1_prostitute-boston-police-police-officer.

[2] Laura Augustín, "Big Claims, Little Evidence: Sweden's Law against Buying Sex," The Local, July 23, 2010, accessed July 25, 2011, http://www.thelocal.se/27962/20100723.

## Chapter 9: So Hott

[1] Jen-E's Blog, "The Statement I Wrote to the Judge . . . R.I.P. Emily (Jordan)," accessed August 25, 2011, http://www.myspace.com/peytonanna/blog/127160103.

[2] Manny Fernandez, "Prostitutes' Disappearances Were Noticed Only When the First Bodies Were Found," *New York Times*, April 7, 2011, accessed August 27, 2011, http://www.nytimes.com/2011/04/08/nyregion/08bodies.html.

[3] Ibid.

[4] Ibid.

[5] Associated Press, "Judge Criticized for Considering Gang Rape of Prostitute 'Theft of Services,'" Fox News.com, November 1, 2007, accessed August 29, 2011, http://www.foxnews.com/story/0,2933,307245,00.html#ixzz1GaoVSh7x.

[6] Ibid.

[7] Jose Antonio Vargas and Darryl Fears, "At Least 3 Percent of D.C. Residents Have HIV or AIDS, City Study Finds; Rate Up 22% from 2006," *Washington Post*, March 15, 2009, accessed February 29, 2012, http://www.washingtonpost.com/wp-dyn/content/article/2009/03/14/AR2009031402176.html.

[8] "Global HIV and AIDS Estimates, End of 2009," Avert, http://www.avert.org/worldstats.htm.

[9] Elizabeth Pisani, *The Wisdom of Whores: Bureaucrats, Brothels, and the Business of AIDS* (New York: W. W. Norton, 2008), 135.

## Chapter 11: American Woman

[1] James O. Prochaska, John Norcross, and Carlo DiClemente, *Changing for Good: A Revolutionary Six-Stage Program for Overcoming Bad Habits and Moving Your Life Positively Forward* (New York: Avon Books, 1994).

## Chapter 12: Your Own Personal Jesus

[1] "Principles of Harm Reduction," Harm Reduction Coalition, accessed April 8, 2011, http://www.harmreduction.org/section.php?id=62.

[2] "Mission Statement," Helping Individual Prostitutes Survive (HIPS), accessed April 7, 2011, http://hips.org.

[3] "About Us," SWOP-USA: Sex Workers Outreach Project, accessed April 23, 2011, http://www.swopusa.org/en/about.

[4] Elizabeth Pisani, *The Wisdom of Whores: Bureaucrats, Brothels, and the Business of AIDS* (New York: W. W. Norton, 2008).